Beds and Bedroom Furniture

Beds and Bedroom Furniture

The Best Of Fine WoodWorking

The Taunton Press

Cover photo by Alec Waters

BOOKS & VIDEOS

for fellow enthusiasts

First printing: 1997
Printed in the United States of America

A FINE WOODWORKING Book

FINE WOODWORKING® is a trademark of The Taunton Press, Inc.,
registered in the U.S. Patent and Trademark Office.

The Taunton Press, Inc.
63 South Main Street
P.O. Box 5506
Newtown, Connecticut 06470-5506

Library of Congress Cataloging-in-Publication Data

Beds and bedroom furniture : the best of Fine woodworking.
    p. cm.
    Includes index.
    ISBN 1-56158-191-7
    1. Bedroom furniture 2. Furniture making
 I. Fine woodworking.
TT197.5.B4B43   1997
684.1–dc20
                              96-35220
                                CIP

Contents

Introduction

Few pieces of furniture we own are as personal as those in our bedrooms. Bureaus, beds, and small bedside tables—no matter what their style or shape—all are personal in a way that even the most beautiful set of kitchen cabinets will never be. Good bedroom furniture does more than give us a place to sleep or provide storage for socks. The best of it has grace and presence, qualities that seem in harmony with its setting.

The authors represented in this collection of *Fine Woodworking* articles build furniture in a variety of styles. Pieces range from Norm Vandal's graceful Queen Anne lowboy that serves as a dressing table to William Turner's spectacular sleigh bed, a challenging bit of woodworking that took 1,200 hours to design and build. In between there are bureaus, cribs, and tables.

In addition to discussions of individual pieces of furniture, these articles also cover techniques that make building them possible. Mac Campbell, for instance, can show you how to make quarter columns to embellish a chest of drawers. John Byers explains how to coax a curved chest out of flat stock. Christian Becksvoort's method for installing drawer stops in a bureau or chest helps guarantee that drawers will sit flush to the case—permanently.

You'll find something here to grace just about any bedroom, whatever style it might be.

—Scott Gibson, editor

The "Best of *Fine Woodworking*" series spans more than 12 years of *Fine Woodworking* magazine. There is no duplication between these books and the popular "*Fine Woodworking* on..." series. A footnote with each article gives the date of first publication; product availability, suppliers' addresses, and prices may have changed since then.

Traditional details suit a modern bed design. *The simple shapes and light component sizes of this bed's cherry frame allow it to be easily situated in any bedroom. Whether the size is king, queen, full or twin (as shown here), the authors prefer this same basic box-spring-less construction. A sheet of ³/₄-in. melamine, resting on slats, supports the bed's mattress.*

Construct a Classic Bed
Flexible frame design allows wood movement and easy take down

by Doug Mooberry and Steve Latta

W e build four-poster bed frames using the same basic construction that has held together for over 200 years: Mortise-and-tenon joinery connects the head and foot rails to the posts; both side- and end-rail tenons are held in their post mortises by bed bolts and nuts. This lets us easily assemble and knockdown the frame, and it allows us to tighten up the joints when the wood moves. To improve the traditional construction methods, we use modern tools and production techniques when shaping components and cutting joinery. And unlike a conventional bed frame that supports the mattress on a box spring, we prefer a different mattress-suspension system, which eliminates the box spring and allows us greater design opportunities (see the photo on the facing page).

We came up with a way to support a mattress on a sheet of melamine, which rests on slats (see the drawing on p. 10). Then we can downsize the rails because they no longer have to cover a box spring (see the near right photo). This construction, called a platform bed, permits the rails to be located higher on the post, which enables more shaping of the leg section. Having higher rails also makes it easier to clean under the bed, and you're less likely to knock your shins when you get into the bed. While discussing the frame design we use, including how we allow for headboard wood movement, we'll describe the setups we use to simplify and speed up the bed-building process in our shop.

Bed design

Before we mill any wood for a bed, we completely work up the design with the customer, offering historical research when necessary. It's important that the post style and headboard shape complement the existing furniture of a bedroom (see the photo on the facing page). To get traditional ideas, we often look in antique magazines, museums and Wallace Nutting's *Furniture Treasury* (Macmillan Publishing Co., Inc., 866 Third Ave., New York, N.Y. 10022; 1933). For contemporary ideas, we look at old *Design Books* (The Taunton Press) or in back issues of *Architectural Digest*. We never just reproduce a bed, though. By refining proportions, using unusually figured wood or choosing a special finish, we can significantly improve a bed's appearance.

We encourage customers to order platform beds (those without box springs). There are other reasons to eliminate the box spring besides the disadvantages pre-

Box spring or not? These foot rail-to-post assemblies (above) are similar. However, the mahogany frame (front) requires a box spring while the maple frame (rear) does not. Because the left assembly's rails do not have to cover a box spring, they can be narrower and located higher on the post, which allows better shaping of the leg.

You can create a wide range of turned or shaped bed posts (right). Here are a sampling of post sizes and styles in cherry. From the left: New England traditional (yet to be finished), country Sheraton, fluted Chippendale, pencil post and contemporary (with a bed-bolt hole showing).

viously mentioned. First, box springs cost money. Second, you may need to hang a ruffle to disguise the box spring or to make the bedspread look right (a frame without a box spring allows you to extend the mattress over the rails, so the covers hang nicely). Third, box springs make moving a challenge. Just ask any mover who has confronted a curved stairway with a queen-sized bed.

Our platform beds get their influence from early 18th-century beds. This style remained popular up through the late 1700s. At that time, Thomas Sheraton developed "field beds," which were used in military tents because the frames could be easily disassembled and relocated. Aside from their ability to knock down, the best feature of a bolt-together bed is its versatility. By swapping different post styles (see the photo at right above), we've made everything from traditional canopy beds to contemporary low-post beds—in sizes from twin to king. (Refer to the chart on p. 11 for overall frame and component dimensions based on typical mattress sizes).

Stock preparation

After we've arrived at a bed's size and style, the next step is to measure the mattress exactly. We once built a bed from dimensions that were given to us by a mattress salesman. Because he gave us the wrong height, we wound up with a bed whose headboard barely showed above the pillows. Now we always measure the mattress twice, and we usually yell at the salesman once. This is also the time we order the bed hardware, such as bed bolts and their covers (available from Ball & Ball, 463 W. Lincoln Highway, Exton, Pa. 19341; 215-363-7330 or Horton Brasses Inc., Nooks Hill Road, P.O. Box 95, Cromwell, Conn. 06416; 203-635-4400)

Depending on what a customer prefers, we usually select bed-frame stock from wood stored in our barn. We use common hardwoods like cherry, maple, walnut and mahogany. Generally, we allow thick green wood to dry a year to reach about 13% moisture content before we kiln-dry it. We make sure that all four bed posts come from the same log (glued up posts

Bed frame options

These two basic bed frames support their mattresses on melamine resting on slats. The two headboard-to-post connections (see details A & B) show how the frames handle wood movement. Like a conventional box spring bed frame, the posts and rails assemble with bed bolts (see detail C).

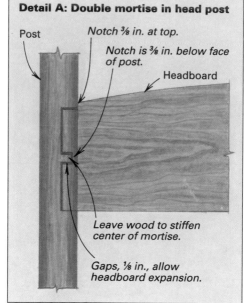

Detail A: Double mortise in head post

Post

Notch ⅜ in. at top.

Notch is ⅜ in. below face of post.

Headboard

Leave wood to stiffen center of mortise.

Gaps, ⅛ in., allow headboard expansion.

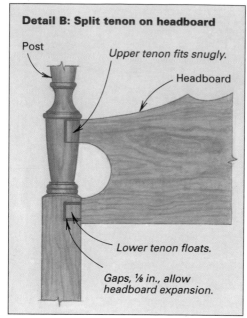

Detail B: Split tenon on headboard

Post

Upper tenon fits snugly.

Headboard

Lower tenon floats.

Gaps, ⅛ in., allow headboard expansion.

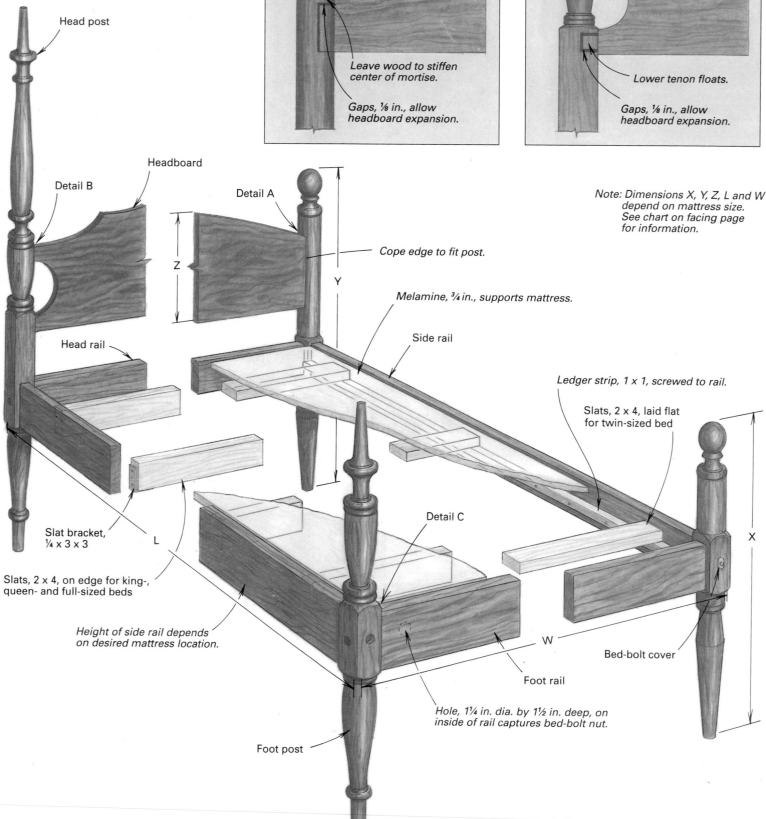

Head post

Headboard

Detail B

Head rail

Slat bracket, ¼ x 3 x 3

L

Slats, 2 x 4, on edge for king-, queen- and full-sized beds

Height of side rail depends on desired mattress location.

Foot post

Detail A

Z

Cope edge to fit post.

Y

Melamine, ¾ in., supports mattress.

Side rail

Detail C

W

Foot rail

Hole, 1¼ in. dia. by 1½ in. deep, on inside of rail captures bed-bolt nut.

Note: Dimensions X, Y, Z, L and W depend on mattress size. See chart on facing page for information.

Ledger strip, 1 x 1, screwed to rail.

Slats, 2 x 4, laid flat for twin-sized bed

X

Bed-bolt cover

Drawings: Lee Hov

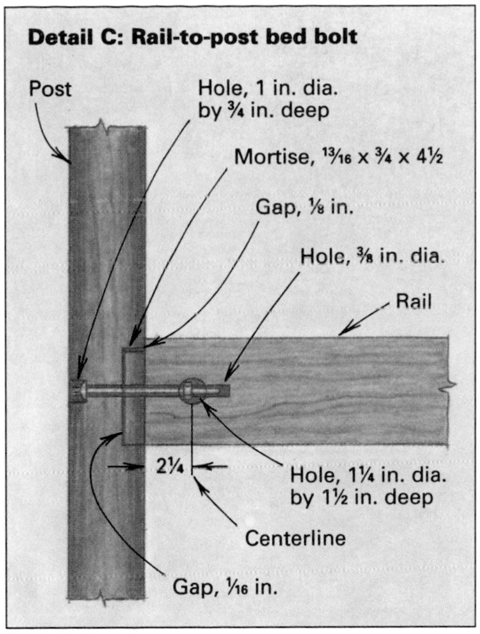
Detail C: Rail-to-post bed bolt
Post
Hole, 1 in. dia. by ¾ in. deep
Mortise, 13/16 x ¾ x 4½
Gap, ⅛ in.
Hole, ⅜ in. dia.
Rail
2¼
Hole, 1¼ in. dia. by 1½ in. deep
Centerline
Gap, 1/16 in.

Bed proportions

Mattress size ✱ (w x l)	King (76 x 80)	Queen (60 x 80)	Full (54 x 75)	Twin (39 x 75)
Length of side rails ◆	80½	80½	75½	75½
Length of head and foot rails ◆◗	73½	56½	50½	37
Head-post height (Y)✚				
Top	24	22	20	17
Block	6	6	6	5
Leg	14	14	14	14
Foot-post height (X)✚				
Top	9	9	9	9
Block	6	6	6	5
Leg	14	14	14	14
Post section (square)✚	2¾ to 3½	2¾ to 3½	2¾ to 3½	2¾ to 3½
Rail section (w x t)✚	5 x 1¾	5 x 1¾	5 x 1¾	4 x 1¾
Headboard width (Z)✚	20	18	16	13

Notes:
- ◆ Length of rails includes tenons.
- ✱ Frames shown require no box spring. Mattress sizes shown are industry standards.
- ✚ Post, rail and headboard sizes are for traditional bed (see photo on p. 36).
- ◗ Add two rail thicknesses to frame width if you want mattress inset from rails.

are unacceptable in our shop). In addition, we carefully match the headboard stock to the posts, and we try to select rail stock that is similar in grain and color to the posts. Next we rough-cut the stock, allowing extra length for rail tenons and for parting off posts if they're to be turned. Then we let the stock sit in the shop a while before we mill it.

Frame construction

The mattress-suspension system we use begins with 2x4 slats; three laid on their side for a twin bed, four laid on edge for a double or queen and five on edge for a king-sized bed. To hold up the slats on a twin frame, we screw a ledger strip around the interior of the rails (see the drawing on the facing page). For larger beds, we install slat-hanging brackets (angle iron) above the bottom of the rail. On top of the base of slats, we lay a sheet of ¾-in. melamine. The melamine stiffens and squares the frame, supports the mattress and, because it is smooth, prevents the mattress cover from tearing. We screw the slats to the brackets so that the top of the melamine lies at or just below the top of the rails.

Posts—Each post has three sections: the leg, the block and the top. The leg likes to be at least 14 in. long to allow for proper shaping (see the photo at left on p. 9) and to strengthen the rail connection by reducing the lever-arm of the upper post. The center block needs to be at least 1 in. longer than the rail height (longer if you want to shape transitional lamb's tongues). The block size should also look proportionate to the rest of the post (see the photo at right on p. 9). The top section of the post carries the headboard and is the most visible area of the bed. To figure the length of the top of a head post, we place headboard and post patterns against the stock to make sure the connection will occur at a sensible place. To figure the length of foot posts, we mark the posts a couple of inches above where the mattress top will be.

We send 90% of our bed posts to local turner Mark Taylor to do the shaping. Along with stock for the posts, we give him a full-scale pattern showing the spindle design. Once the posts have been shaped, we determine the rail height. Then we lay out the center of the mortises on the correct faces of the post. We extend a bottom line around all the faces to use as a reference line for drilling bed-bolt holes later (see drawing detail C above).

To waste the bed-post mortises, you can use a plunge router and the jig shown in the photo below. The jig is easy to construct and is adjustable to fit most posts. We made our jig's base out of particleboard and poplar, and we capped the rails with hardwood runners. We screwed together plywood and scraps to make the router carriage. If a post is tapered, we insert a couple of shims before clamping it between the jig's rails. Next we double-check each mortise layout because the post is scrap if the location is wrong. Then, using a ½-in., two-spiral end mill (Forest City Tool Co., 620 23rd St. N.W., Hickory,

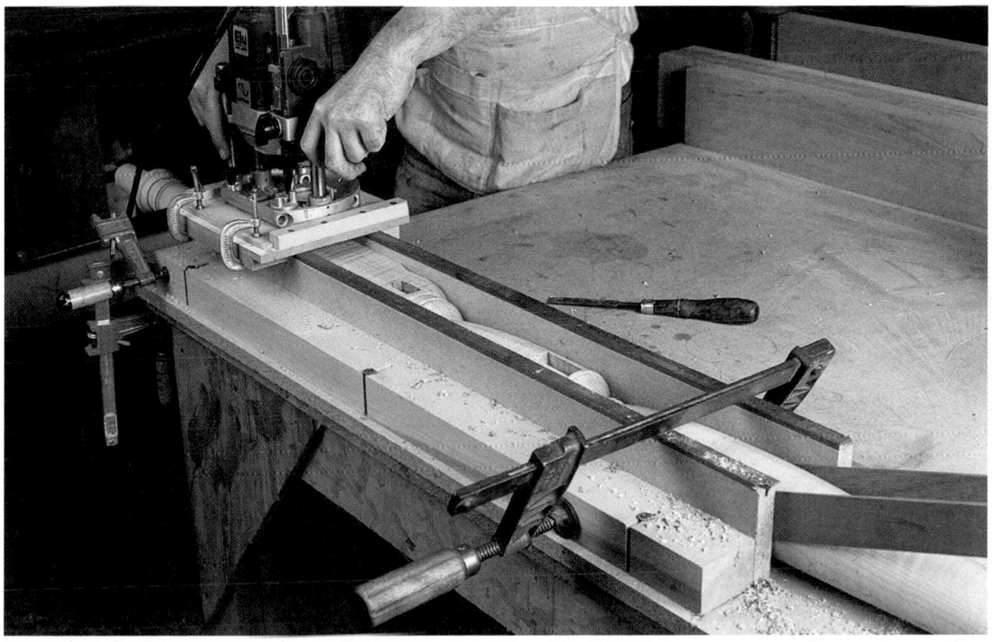

Routing bed-post mortises*—With a post wedged in this jig, you can easily rout mortises for the rail tenons whether the post is turned or shaped. Then just use a chisel to square the mortises' corners. For adjustability, the router base slides in tracks in the carriage, and one of the jig's rails has slots for its mounting screws.*

NC 28601; 704-322-4266), we rout one side of the mortise, rotate the setup 180° and rout the other side. Although the bit leaves rounded ends, it's quick and easy to square the mortises with a hand chisel.

Rails—After we dimension the rails, we cut their tenons on a radial-arm saw fitted with a 10-in. dado head. To prevent transferring inaccuracies from slightly bowed or twisted stock, we space out the work from the saw's fence, and we butt the end of the rail against a pointed stop (see the top photo below). The stop contacts the same (center) spot on the rail when we flip it to cut the other cheek. To ensure a snug fit in the mortises, we cut the tenons thick, and we shave them down with a rabbet plane. After we have cleaned up the shoulders, we set the rail on edge, raise the sawblade and then notch ⅝-in. on the top (but not the bottom) of the tenon. The notch allows the rail to expand and contract without exposing the post mortise. This orientation also helps us to tell which side of the rail is up during assembly (see drawing detail C on the previous page).

Headboard—Because headboards are wide, lots of wood movement will occur. Cutting a long mortise to accept a slightly under-width tenon will handle the problem, but it's likely that the mortise will open up and leave an unsightly gap where the headboard meets the post. Therefore, we allow for expansion and contraction at the (cross grain) post-to-headboard joints by doing one of two things: We either shape a double mortise (leaving a center section of wood to stiffen the mortise) and notch the headboard ends to form twin tenons (see the drawing detail A on p. 10), or we split the tenons on the headboard and undersize the lower tenons, so they float in their post mortises (as shown in drawing detail B on p. 10).

With split-tenon headboards, we lay out the tenons so that the lower one falls onto a flat and the upper (snug) tenon falls just under a bead or other detail. Tapering the ¹³⁄₁₆-in. headboard thickness on the tenons ensures that they'll fit tightly into the ¾-in.-wide post mortises. We cope both the top and bottom of the lower tenons, so the mortises will be covered no matter which

way the wood moves. If we use a double-mortise, we undersize both of the tenons, notch the top of the headboard and cope the shoulder to fit the post. This enables the wood to move without being seen.

To form the shape of a headboard, we make a full-scale template out of medium-density fiberboard (MDF). Each template, which we keep, is half of a headboard: We trace the left side, and then flip it to get the right side. This lets us fudge the length of a headboard, such as for larger bed frames. After we score the shape on the stock with an Exacto knife, we sabersaw close to the line. Then we clamp the pattern to the stock and flush-trim the shape using a bearing-guided router bit. To prevent tearout, we always rout down the headboard's slope.

Bed bolts—Because we use authentic bed bolts in our frames, we provide the customer with a traditional wrench when we deliver the bed. We lay out the bed-bolt holes so the bolts will clear each other inside the post. A ½ in. offset spacing works well because this lets us hang adjacent bed-bolt covers at the same height. Boring the holes is a three-step process: First, we bore a hole in the post to recess the bolt head. The hole is large enough to fit the bed-bolt wrench, but small enough to be hidden by a bed-bolt cover. Second, we bore a 1½-in.-deep hole in the side of the rail (to house the nut), using a 1¼-in. Forstner bit chucked in our drill press. Having a rounded seat for the nut instead of a flat allows greater adjustment when it comes time to assemble the frame (see the bottom right photo). And third, using the post hole as a guide, we center-bore a ⅜-in. hole (slightly larger than the bolt) through the post into the rail end using a 10-in.-long twist bit. To do this, we lay the post on its side, fit the tenon in its mortise, mark the mating parts on the inside with a punch, and then bore the hole with a hand drill (see the bottom left photo). If the layout is accurate, the bit will emerge in the center of the nut hole. We continue drilling into the rail to provide enough depth for the entire bed bolt (see the drawing detail C on p. 11).

We assemble the posts, headboard and rails before we sand and finish the frame. Once on site, we loosely assemble the frame and install the melamine, which squares up the frame. Then we snug all the bed bolts and lay down the mattress. □

Sawing bed-rail tenons—A 10-in. dado set in the radial-arm saw makes quick work of tenons. To ensure proper registration on bowed rail stock, the authors screwed a spacer block to the left fence (with clearance for the guard), and they shaped the right stop so that it contacts only the center of the tenon end.

Boring bed-bolt holes—Steve Latta drills through a post into the end of a rail (see example at right). The post hole is counter-bored for the bed-bolt head (foreground).

Assembling the head of the bed—After Latta loosely tightens the bed bolts between the head rail and posts (bottom), he checks the fit of the headboard.

Doug Mooberry and Steve Latta build beds and other furniture at Kinloch Woodworking in Unionville, Pa.

Designing a Captain's Bed

Launching a commission with the right details and hardware

by Arnold d'Epagnier

Ten years and ten moves later, Gail's captain's bed is still the safe haven for her that it was when I built it. When she commissioned the bed, Gail was going through a difficult period in her life. Listening to her describe the bed she wanted me to build, I began to realize that she wanted something more than just a queen-sized bed with some storage space below. She was asking for an embodiment of permanence and stability. Reading between the lines of a customer's requests and getting to the essence of what that person really wants is never easy. But I felt confident with this commission because I knew Gail well and because I already had a design in mind that would meet all of her requirements—both voiced and implied.

I'd been thinking about captain's beds for a while, waiting for an opportunity to bring together in wood the vague elements of the bed as it existed in my mind. I sketched a bed with high headboard and footboard and sides sweeping up to meet them. Its shape evoked a cabin-like atmosphere, cozy and secure. I showed Gail those rough sketches, we discussed them and I made some minor revisions. After working through some final details, I came up with drawings for, and then built, the bed shown in the photo below. Although the stormy seas have long since subsided (Gail's happily married now, with a baby daughter), the warm hue of the mahogany and the bed's cradling curves still beckon, offering solace and peaceful repose.

Massive but refined, *this captain's bed achieves its grace through simple but effective details. The bed combines a well-built, inconspicuous drawer system with bold, shopmade hardware and subtle stylistic details that evoke nautical images.*

From *Fine Woodworking* (November 1992) 97:53-55

Design challenges

This project had three design challenges: I needed to lighten the bed visually to counterbalance its mass and solidity with a little grace; I needed a means of connecting the massive frame-and-panel headboard to the side rails that would take into account their differences in wood movement; and I needed a durable, convenient drawer system that would look integral to the bed rather than added on.

One of my main influences as a furniture designer is the simple, elegant work of Charles and Henry Greene, early 20th-century architect-builders whose work has come to define the Arts and Crafts movement in America. The Greene brothers' overall sense of proportion and the characteristic soft, radiused edges of their furniture strike me as quietly dignified, having a well-bred self-assurance. Because I was building a captain's bed, I wanted to lighten the bed's visual mass and to add some nautical influence to my Greene and Greene design vocabulary. I designed the headboard as a frame-and-panel unit with the panel consisting of a number of beveled-edge tonguc-in-groove boards reminiscent of lapstrake wooden boats. Also, because the panel is composed of a number of parts, rather than one large panel, its apparent mass is diminished. The middle board of the panel, though beveled along its edges and grooved to appear multipartite, is actually one long board tenoned into the frame, adding rigidity.

I was able to lighten the feel of the bed further, and to soften its geometry, by sweeping the sides down from headboard and footboard and by scalloping the bottom edge of the rails, headboard and footboard. This also adds top-to-bottom symmetry to each part of the bed and provides ventilation for the mattress and bed linens. The human body gives off roughly a quart of water each night, some of which evaporates and some of which is absorbed by the mattress and linens. Adequate ventilation makes for a better rest and a longer mattress life. The routed slots in the bed's sides and footboard also help with ventilation, reassert the Greenes' influence and lighten the bed's look.

Shopmade hardware resolves design dilemma

Given the headboard's height (over 3 ft.), a single bed bolt at each corner would have been inadequate. I didn't want to use two or three bolts at each corner because that would've made the bed a pain to assemble and disassemble, and I didn't trust the drop-style rail connectors with so large and heavy a headboard and footboard. Seizing upon the situation as an opportunity rather than a dilemma, I decided to make my own brass hardware. Although

Three angles hold the headboard in and one keeps the rail in place. Unable to find any satisfactory off-the-shelf hardware, the author made his own. Using conventional woodworking equipment, he cut and shaped the brass angle to come up with this unique bed hardware system. He mortised the brass-wear plates on the inside to prevent injury or discomfort resulting from rubbing up against blunt brass edges.

many suppliers aren't interested in selling small quantities of brass, generally you can find a cooperative company or get some through a scrap yard. I purchased my brass angle from C-S Metals Service, Inc. (7325 Washington Blvd., Baltimore, Md. 21227; 410-796-5661); they will also sell you stainless steel, aluminum and other metals in small quantities.

After a little head scratching, I came up with the solution in the photo at left. I sandwiched the headboard between the shoulders of vertical rabbets in the rails and three brass angles bolted through the rails. I mortised the brass plates on the inside (which function as washers) flush with the wood (see the photo below) because bodily contact with the brass is likely, and I didn't want any hard or sharp edges exposed.

The top angles at either end of the headboard are screwed into the back of the headboard; they hold in the top of the rails. Dovetailed support slats (for a box spring or a firmness board) drop into the ledger strip to hold the rails at the proper distance (see the photo below). The footboard, a single, large glued-up board, is connected to the rails with angles similar in appearance to those used at the headboard, but the angles are simply bolted through both rails and footboard because their grain is oriented horizontally.

Brass is soft enough to machine with woodworking tools. I used my tablesaw (with a carbide-tipped blade in it) to cut the angle to size and a bandsaw with a bimetal blade to cut the arcs at the angle's ends. Be absolutely sure to wear eye protection when working brass (preferably a full-face shield) and long sleeves as well. After cutting the brass angle to size and cutting the arcs, I ground off all the sharp edges and filed the sides and edges smooth. I marked the locations for screw holes using a template and a steel transfer punch and then drilled the holes with a standard steel bit. The net effect of my shopmade bed hardware system is a rigid, sturdy frame, which allows for wood movement and enhances the nautical motif suggested by the headboard.

Underbed storage

I wanted the drawers beneath the bed to be as inconspicuous as possible, so I cut the drawer fronts from the middle board in the main part of each rail, thus keeping the grain unbroken except for the width of the sawkerf. The width of this board determines the height of the drawer. When gluing up the rails, I used waxed paper to keep glue off the edges of the drawer fronts and duct tape to hold them in place.

To keep the contents of the drawers relatively dust-free (partic-

Photos: Vincent Laurence; drawings: David Dann

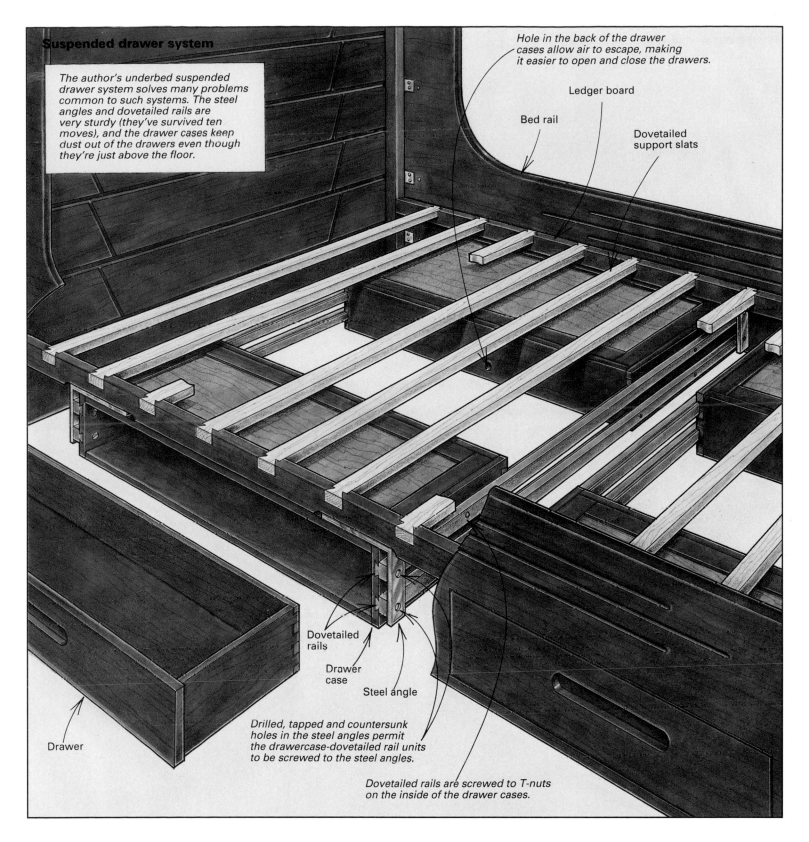

Suspended drawer system

The author's underbed suspended drawer system solves many problems common to such systems. The steel angles and dovetailed rails are very sturdy (they've survived ten moves), and the drawer cases keep dust out of the drawers even though they're just above the floor.

Hole in the back of the drawer cases allow air to escape, making it easier to open and close the drawers.

Ledger board

Bed rail

Dovetailed support slats

Dovetailed rails

Drawer case

Steel angle

Drilled, tapped and countersunk holes in the steel angles permit the drawercase-dovetailed rail units to be screwed to the steel angles.

Drawer

Dovetailed rails are screwed to T-nuts on the inside of the drawer cases.

ularly because they're so close to the floor), I housed the drawers in cases rather than using simple runners or a web frame. The drawer cases are slid onto dovetailed rails and screwed into place, flush against the inside of the bed rails. The drawer cases are ⅛ in. smaller all around than the opening in the bed rail, and the drawer front extends ⅛ in. past the drawer sides, so the cases act as flush stops for the drawer fronts.

Pairs of dovetailed runners on either side of the four drawer cases are screwed to steel angles, which I tapped (see the drawing above) for ¼-20 machine screws. I screwed the angles into shallow mortises on the bottom of the ledger strip on both sides of the bed.

Little details can make the difference between a merely satisfied customer and one who will commission furniture from me again. I try not to overlook any small touches. I made sure to drill holes in the backs of the drawer cases to allow air to escape. Otherwise, it could be difficult to open or close the drawers. Also, I made a drop-in toe kick (four boards with half-laps cut near their ends) to cut down on dust buildup beneath the bed. Finally, and in the same vein, the last thing I did before finishing the bed with a few coats of oil was to sign it. I carved my name discretely into the back side of the headboard, satisfied to let posterity be the judge of my handiwork. □

Arnold d'Epagnier is a custom furnituremaker in Colesville, Md.

Making a Sheraton Bed

The challenge is in the posts

by Philip C. Lowe

Turned posts are the most dramatic feature of a Sheraton bed. The posts can be turned in one piece, as the author did here, or turned in two or more pieces, which are glued together later.

Beds often are very simple, even if they look as complicated as the Sheraton bed in the photo on the facing page. The joinery isn't complicated, and there aren't many parts. In fact, once you've made the posts for this bed, the hard work is behind you. Think about the posts as different circular-shaped moldings stacked on top of one another. The posts can be made in one piece, as I do, or made in several pieces, which are glued together later. The posts also can be made without decorative reeding, which cuts out many hours of work on the project and still results in a pleasing design.

I always make full-scale drawings for pieces that I'm about to make. For this bed, I have to draw only one of the posts, half the shape of the headboard and the joinery detail for the rail-post connection. I use the drawing to make a story stick (a scrap of wood where dimensions and pro-files are marked), so laying out the bed posts is both easy and accurate.

Mounting the blank

The bedpost blanks are milled to 3½ in. sq. from 16/4 stock and rough cut to length, leaving a couple of inches at each end for mounting in the lathe. Turning the full-length blanks is no problem on my lathe, with its 10-ft.-long bed. But if you don't have this luxury, you will have to turn the

Sheraton bed: *Posts can be turned from a single length of wood or made in pieces and glued together later.*

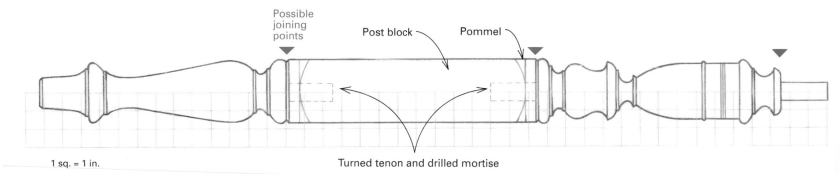

Possible joining points

Post block

Pommel

Turned tenon and drilled mortise

1 sq. = 1 in.

Photos: Charley Robinson; drawing: Kathleen Rushton

A Sheraton-style bed is easy to make, despite its complicated appearance. Reeding is time-consuming, but optional, and the joinery is straightforward. On this bed, the author skipped the reeding on the less-prominent headboard posts.

Use a story stick to lay out accurate and consistent turning details. And the story stick is a handy reference when turning because the shape and diameter of each post section is drawn right on it.

post in sections, and join them together by boring a hole in one part and turning a mating tenon on the adjoining member. The joints should be cemented with yellow glue or epoxied for extra strength. I've marked a few joining points, as shown in the drawing below. As a rule, the best place to join these parts is at a fillet above or below a cove, torus or ogee shape.

I mount the blank at the headstock end with a faceplate and plywood disc drive center, which provides a more positive drive than a spur center. This arrangement also lets me add an indexing wheel (see the box on p. 19) and makes it easy to remount the blank.

The drive center is a circular piece of ¾-in.-thick plywood screwed to the faceplate. The plywood has a square hole the size of the turning blank cut out of its center. To mount the blank, one end is slipped into the square hole, and the ball-bearing center in the tailstock is slid into position at the opposite end and locked in place.

Turning the posts

The first step is to locate the post block, which is the non-turned section of the post into which the side and end rails are mortised. I scribe shoulder lines around the post, and with a backsaw, cut kerfs on all four corners at the shoulder points. The kerfs prevent the square edges of the post

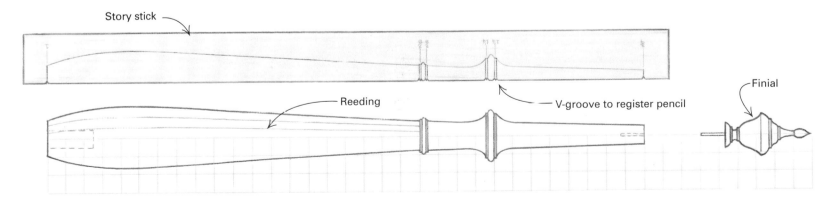

Story stick

Reeding

V-groove to register pencil

Finial

Drilling holes for bed bolts. *Holes bored*
through the bedposts serve as guides when
drilling rails for the bed bolts. The nut is
hidden in a mortise in the side of the rail.

block from chipping when I turn the adjacent sections. After turning the post to the largest possible cylinder above and below the post block, I lay out and turn the pommels (the curved shoulders at the top and bottom of the post block).

To lay out the elements of the posts, I make up two story sticks or rods, one for the section above and one for the section below the post block. On the story sticks, I draw half the profile of the post and mark the diameter of each design element. I cut notches into the edge of the story stick with a skew chisel to make sure the pencil references are made from the same spot when each of the four posts is laid out.

I usually hold the story stick against the revolving blank to scribe the post. Another method is to mark the post with the story stick, as shown in the photo at right on p. 17. Then turn on the lathe, and hold the pencil point at the mark to extend the reference line completely around the post.

I shape the bottom of the post first, turning the cylindrical blank down to the diameters indicated on the story stick with a parting tool. I check each blank's diameter with calipers. Then I shape the curves and hollows with skews and gouges, leaving the cove or scotia cuts for last. Because the

coves create the smallest diameters, leaving these cuts until the end helps to reduce vibration while turning the rest of the post.

The upper section of the post is turned in the same fashion, except I add a steady rest, as shown in the photo on p. 16, to help prevent the post from vibrating and being thrown out of round when turning. After I've turned this section to as accurate a cylinder as possible, I locate the steady rest at the bulbous section of the reeded portion of the post. With the steady rest in place, the upper section is turned to shape, again leaving the coves till last.

Once I've turned the posts to shape, I sand them, starting with 120-grit and working up to 220-grit. Between each sanding, I wet the post and let it dry to raise the grain. I sand everything but the section of post to be carved with reeds because the sanding grit would get in the pores of the wood and dull my carving tool.

Reeding the posts

Because it takes about four hours to carve the reeds into each post, clients frequently choose to save money by eliminating the reeding entirely or by having just the posts of the footboard reeded, as shown in the photo at left on p. 17. Usually, these posts

are prominently displayed near the middle of the room, and the headboard posts are generally pushed against a wall.

I've found the easiest way to lay out and carve the reeds is right on the lathe. To do this, though, you need an indexing wheel to hold the post in position for scribing the layout lines and carving the reeds. This is a standard feature on some lathes, but not mine, so I added one, as discussed in the box on the facing page.

I also made a scribe for drawing the layout lines. The scribe rides on the lathe's bed and has a pencil set to the center height of the lathe. I mark one reed, as shown in the photo above right, rotate the post and mark another until the post is completely laid out. I use a V-carving tool to carve lines into the post and a series of straight and back-bent gouges to carve the reeds to their half-round shapes. When carving is complete, I sand the reeds.

Putting it all together

After taking the post from the lathe, I drill a hole in the top of the post for a pin that will hold the finial in place and lay out and cut the mortises. There are two on each post block to accept the tenons for the rails and two more in each headboard post.

Indexing wheels for the lathe

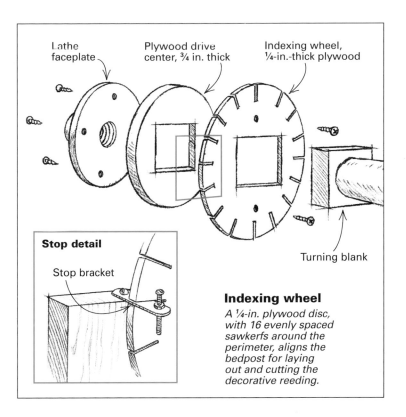

Lathe faceplate

Plywood drive center, ¾ in. thick

Indexing wheel, ¼-in.-thick plywood

Turning blank

Stop detail

Stop bracket

Indexing wheel

A ¼-in. plywood disc, with 16 evenly spaced sawkerfs around the perimeter, aligns the bedpost for laying out and cutting the decorative reeding.

The holes for the bed bolts are staggered, so the bolt for the end rail doesn't interfere with the bolt for the side rail. These ⅜-in.-dia. holes have a 1-in.-dia. counterbore to bury the head of the bolt. I bore the holes on the drill press, starting with the 1-in.-dia. counterbore and then the ⅜-in.-dia. bolt hole, aligning the bit with the center point of the counterbored hole.

I hand drill the bolt holes into the ends of the rails, using the holes in the posts as a guide, as shown in the photo at left on the facing page. Mortises for the nuts are cut into the sides of the rails, so they intersect the bolt holes. ☐

Philip Lowe designs, makes and restores fine furniture in Beverly, Mass.

Turning a bedpost

VIDEO TAKES

Philip Lowe makes a reed-ed post for this Sheraton bed in a 28-minute video tape (VHS only). To order, send $10 to The Taunton Press, Order #011046, P.O. Box 5506, Newtown, CT 06470, or call (800) 888-8286.

The faceplate and plywood drive center that I use to turn my bedposts make the perfect mounting system for an indexing wheel. My indexing wheel is made by cutting a hole in the center of a 10-in.-sq. piece of ¼-in.-thick plywood. The hole fits the turning blank.

After laying out the required number of divisions (16 for the bedposts) on the plywood with a compass, I band-sawed the plywood into a 10-in.-dia. circle. And I cut out the center square on the jigsaw.

Around the perimeter of the disc at each division line, I made a bandsaw cut 1 in. in from the edge of the disc. The indexing wheel is now ready to be slipped over the end of the post

Accurate indexing for reeding. A disc of ¼-in. plywood makes an indexing wheel for laying out reeding on the bedposts. The stop is a piece of bandsaw blade mounted even with the lathe center.

and then screwed to the faceplate and disc drive (see the photo at left).

The stop that engages the kerfs on the indexing wheel is simply a discarded piece of bandsaw blade with the teeth ground off. This stop is held even with the centerline of the lathe by an L-shaped plywood bracket, as shown in the drawing above.

To scribe lines or carve the reeding, I pivot the stop into a sawkerf to hold the post in position. To mark or carve the next and each consecutive line, I slide the stop back and rotate the post to the next sawkerf in the wheel. I slide the stop into place and scribe or carve the next division line. —P.L.

Queen Anne style furniture is readily identifiable by a few of its basic elements, such as cabriole legs, scrolled pediments and flame-carved finials. The author borrowed these elements and applied them to the design of his contemporary Queen Anne bedroom set shown here.

Contemporary Queen Anne
Designing a bedroom set with period elements

by Larry Dern

In the 10 years that I've been designing and building furniture, I have consciously tried not to lock myself into a particular design style. My goal has been to develop the ability and flexibility to design for a variety of tastes and decors. Nonetheless, a majority of my commissions have been for contemporary furniture with clean lines and a minimum of applied details or moldings. However, I was given the opportunity to work with a whole new set of design elements when commissioned to build a Queen Anne style bedroom set consisting of a four-poster bed, a tall chest and a pair of night tables (shown in the photos above).

The furniture was for a new house overlooking Humboldt Bay, near Arcata, Cal., built by friends of mine, Bill and Dottie Haukenberry. The 10-ft.-high ceilings, spacious rooms, covered porches, scrolled corbels (rafter support brackets), detailed custom trim work and the grand Honduras mahogany staircase all combine to give the house an elegantly classic yet contemporary look: a style the owners call Southern Victorian. As avid antique collectors, the Haukenberrys had already decided on Queen Anne style furniture for the 24-ft. by 40-ft. master bedroom, but they weren't able to find what they wanted commercially. So they asked me to design a bedroom set using my contemporary interpretation of the Queen Anne style to fit in with the modern amenities of the house.

To get a feel for Queen Anne style, I visited furniture stores and checked out library books on antique furniture (see *FWW* #87, pp. 73-75). Then I began sketching the pieces, accounting

for the functional requirements of the case pieces and incorporating Queen Anne elements, like cabriole legs, scalloped aprons, broken scrolled pediments and flame-carved finials. Aside from practical and stylistic considerations, I also had to proportion the pieces so they wouldn't be lost in the large, high-ceiling room. I call the resulting designs contemporary Queen Anne; they are unmistakably Queen Anne in appearance, but far from being reproductions.

Blending the period with the practical—The sides of case pieces built during the Queen Anne period were nearly always made from wide solid boards. I decided not to follow this style because I knew that these solid sides also nearly always split due to seasonal expansion and contraction. Instead I used cope-and-stick frames and raised-panel sides for the tall chest and the night tables. Another major break with tradition was using doors on the upper portion of the tall chest instead of running drawers all the way up. This was done for practicality because the top drawers become rather inaccessible; adjustable shelves behind the doors provide more efficient storage. In addition, the raised-panel doors are a unifying element among the pieces, relating to the frame-and-panel sides on all three case pieces and to the two raised-panel doors on each night table (see the drawing).

Using stiles and rails instead of the typical solid wood sides also allowed for full web-frame construction between drawers without restricting the side panels. The horizontal frame members in the

Photos: Sandor Nagyszalanczy; drawing: Aaron Azevedo

front are mortised and tenoned into the leg posts for strength and stability, and the web frames are dadoed into the raised-panel frame stiles on the sides, which in turn are splined to the legs (see the detail in the drawing). All the drawers, except for the two large bottom drawers on the tall chest, are joined with traditional hand-cut half-blind dovetails and they slide on a maple center guide (see the drawing). The fronts of the two bottom drawers on the tall chest join directly to the sides with sliding dovetails. The sides of these drawers are set in ½ in. from each end of the drawer front to allow clearance for a touch of modern technology: a set of Accuride #3037 drawer slides. The bottom web frame on the tall chest has the traditional dust panel to keep the interior clean.

The characteristically Queen Anne cyma curve gooseneck moldings and the flame-carved finials that cap both the tall chest and the bed visually tie the set together, and create the feel of the period. I eliminated the bonnet top behind the curved pediment on the chest, so it would fit nicely against a wall beneath a sloping ceiling. Since I don't have a vast array of shaper cutters geared to the details of period moldings, many of my design decisions were based on the cutters I had. However, the gooseneck molding is such a unique and prominent feature that I hired friend and wood-turner Joe Cusimano to grind a set of knives to a pattern that I designed and then I ran them on a large shaper at a local millwork shop to form the moldings. I also had Cusimano turn the bed posts after I had mortised them for the headboard, footboard and side rails. When I assembled the king-size bed in my shop, it looked huge with its 7-ft.-tall posts, but it seemed perfectly proportioned against the long north wall of the Haukenberry's high-ceiling room.

Probably the most recognizable element of Queen Anne furniture is the cabriole leg. I knew from the start that the set wouldn't be complete without them. I opted for bracket feet under the tall chest, as opposed to raising it on slender cabriole legs, in order to get the most storage. Fortunately, the night tables were ideal candidates for the lowboy form: low cases raised on cabriole legs. The legs on the night tables are bandsawn from 4x4s and the upper square section extends all the way to the top of the case, which

guarantees a solid base. I didn't carve shells on the knees, which is typical of high-style Queen Anne furniture, because I wanted to preserve the clean, uncluttered look and the simplicity of Country style furniture. Scalloped aprons go with cabriole legs like fish and water, but when researching Queen Anne furniture I noticed many different apron designs. The height and curvature of the leg and knee block, along with the overall proportions of a piece, provide a unique set of criteria for defining the aprons' patterns. I suspect that period cabinetmakers did just as I did and designed the apron curves to provide the best visual effect.

I finished the pieces with three coats of satin varnish and rubbed out the last coat with 0000 steel wool and flax soap. The brass hardware from Garrett Wade (161 Ave. of the Americas, New York, N.Y. 10013) was reproduced from period patterns and complements the clean look of the unstained Eastern black cherry.

This commission presented me with a whole new set of design, engineering and construction problems. The departure in style enabled me to expand the parameters of my design vocabulary, and increased my appreciation of period furniture. It was a challenge I'm glad I had the opportunity to accept. ☐

Larry Dern builds a line of jewelry and desktop boxes, as well as custom furniture, in Trinidad, Cal.

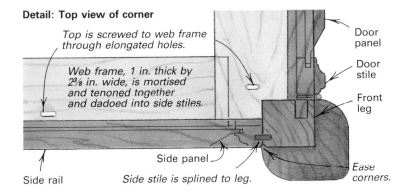

Detail: Top view of corner

Top is screwed to web frame through elongated holes.

Web frame, 1 in. thick by 2⅜ in. wide, is mortised and tenoned together and dadoed into side stiles.

Door panel
Door stile
Front leg

Side panel
Side stile is splined to leg.
Ease corners.
Side rail

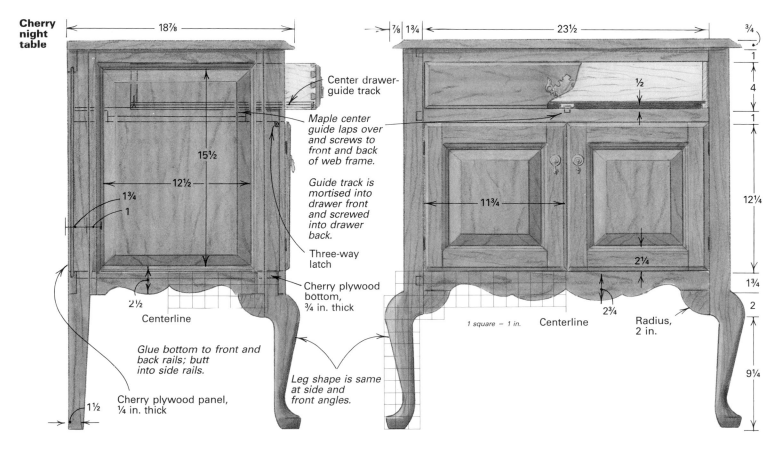

Cherry night table

18⅞

15½

12½

1¾
1

2½

Centerline

Glue bottom to front and back rails; butt into side rails.

Cherry plywood panel, ¼ in. thick

1½

Center drawer-guide track

Maple center guide laps over and screws to front and back of web frame.

Guide track is mortised into drawer front and screwed into drawer back.

Three-way latch

Cherry plywood bottom, ¾ in. thick

Leg shape is same at side and front angles.

⅞ 1¾   23½   ¾

1
4
1

½

11¾

2¼

1 square = 1 in.   Centerline

2¾

Radius, 2 in.

12¼

1¾

2

9¼

This sleigh bed has sufficient detail and variety to challenge any woodworker. But the shopmade fasteners that make the structure rigid yet allow easy disassembly and the basic construction could be used in a more simplified design.

Building a Sleigh Bed
Flowing tambours and intricate detailing enhance a classic design

by William Turner

This sleigh bed is loosely based on an Empire period design by Charles-Honoré Lannier, a 19th-century French cabinetmaker. The bed's stately curves and fine detailing combine to create a striking interplay of both movement and stability. The piece is large and bold. Fully assembled with box spring and mattress, it weighs more than 500 lbs.

Besides being critical to the success of the design, the long, sweeping curves in the headboard and footboard offered the greatest challenge in constructing the bed. I'll discuss the techniques I used and suggest some alternative approaches that could net major savings of both time and effort.

Whatever techniques you choose, the overall construction of the sleigh bed is the same. It consists of three separate elements: The headboard and footboard, which are each made of two curved posts, a crest rail and an internal frame upon which the exterior curved surfaces are mounted; the four rails, which bolt together at their corners; and two foot assemblies that complete the bed. These units are all joined together with threaded rods and anchor bolts, as shown in figure 1 on pp. 24-25, to allow the bed to be disassembled for moving. By separating the headboard and footboard from the feet, I was able to avoid major stress points at the critical rail joints common in more traditional bed assemblies. It also made the bed much more rigid.

Working with treasured rosewood and precious design freedom

The bed, shown in the photo at left, turned out to be one of the most interesting and challenging jobs in my 15 years of building custom furniture. By delivery time, I had logged over 1,200 hours in the design and construction of the piece, and I'd spent more than $3,000 for materials and custom tooling. The keen interest of my client, Mrs. James Totten, daughter of Gen. George Patton, added greatly to my enjoyment of the project. An instant camaraderie, born of shared interests, developed from our first meeting. Early on, Mrs. Totten revealed a stack of milled rosewood boards, 8 in. to 10 in. wide and averaging 8 ft. long, that her late husband had brought back from Brazil some 40 years before. She wanted me to use this wood in the construction of her bed. I felt as if I had stumbled upon a buried treasure and was being offered the job of excavating it. From these early meetings, the job developed its own momentum, and I soon began to appreciate what a long and involved project I was in for.

After receiving preliminary design approval based on quarter-scale drawings, I worked up the full-scale drawings, with details of the construction, joinery and carving, as well as the various edge and surface treatments. Although I make most of my design decisions at this point, I try to keep my options open so that I can make changes as the project progresses. I've found that trying to come up with a firm estimate at this stage really dampens creativity by locking me into my original design ideas. I believe that my best work comes when I'm free to make midcourse corrections, allowing the piece to grow and develop just as the trees from which it is built grow.

Veneering and bolting the four rails together

The rail assembly, to which all other components are bolted, consists of head and foot rails, two side rails and three angle-

The endgrain mahogany edging and carved details highlight the flowing lines of the sleigh bed.

iron slats. The solid-mahogany rails are veneered on the outside with fiddleback mahogany. A large cove molding on top and a continuous band of rosewood along the bottom edge visually connect the bed's headboard and footboard. Oak ledgers screwed to the inside of the rails hold three angle-iron slats. The ledgers and the slats support the box spring and mattress, and the foot assemblies bolt to these ledgers. The four rails are joined by haunched miters and threaded rods.

My sleigh bed was designed around a standard queen-size mattress-and-box spring set; if you're going to make this bed, size components according to the spring-and-mattress set you'll be using. To begin, I cut the solid-mahogany rail stock to length for the side and end rails. Next, I veneered the outside faces of the rails with fiddleback mahogany and the inside faces with plain mahogany to stabilize the construction. The cove molding, which is mortised and glued to the top of the rails, was milled from 2-in.-sq. stock for the side rails and 2-in.-thick by 2½-in.-wide stock for the end rails to accommodate haunched miters, as shown in figure 2 on p. 26. Before cutting the haunched miters, which provide a much stronger joint than standard miter joints, I glued and screwed the 2-in.-sq. oak ledgers to the rails, as shown in figure 2. Then I joined the rails with shopmade fasteners consisting of 5/16-in.-dia. by 3-in.-long threaded brass rods secured with washers and cap nuts. To hide the screws that secure the ledgers, I glued a 1¼-in.-wide band of rosewood into a ⅛-in.-deep rabbet in the outside bottom edge of all the rails. After thoroughly cleaning the rosewood with acetone, I glued it into the rabbets with epoxy. The wood's natural oiliness tends to yield unpredictable results with aliphatic resin (yellow glue).

Carved foot assemblies that carry the load

The feet, with carved scrolls on both the inside and outside surfaces, were dovetailed in pairs to oak stretchers, as shown in figure 2 on p. 26. These foot-and-stretcher units were then bolted through the oak ledgers to the underside of the rail assembly at the head and foot of the bed. I added filler blocks at the ends of the oak ledgers to provide extra width where the bolt holes for the foot assemblies are close to the edge of the ledgers.

Because the bed is so heavy, I was careful to avoid short grain in the curved section when laying out the feet. Also, a carved offset heel on the back edge of each foot moves the floor contact point more directly beneath the load. I cut five 10⅜-in.-long blanks from 4-in.-thick by 10-in.-wide stock for feet; the extra blank was for working out the carving technique. After laying out the shape of the foot and the spirals for the carved volutes on both sides of each blank, the foot's J-shape was roughed out on the bandsaw. The side of the leg was also bandsawn to provide relief for the scroll ends, which rise as they approach the center of the volute. Since time was pressing me, I had good friend and fellow North Bennet Street School graduate Scot Schmidt, of Portsmouth, N.H., carve the feet and the scroll brackets. After gluing the feet to the stretchers that join them together, I drilled and installed anchor bolts, as shown in figure 2 on p. 26.

Shaping and detailing the curved headboard and footboard posts

I believe that the upright posts that form the headboard and footboard are the most

Photos: Rob Karosis; drawings: Bob La Pointe

dramatic and important design elements of the sleigh bed. Their shape and angle define the overall piece—too much rake and the bed begins to resemble a brontosaurus, too little and the sleeping space becomes claustrophobic. Given the importance of these elements, the shaping and detailing of the posts became the most time-consuming aspect of the entire project. Since the only differences between the headboard and footboard are the overall size and shape, I'll limit my discussion to the construction of the headboard.

The framework for the headboard consists of two upright posts connected at the top with a solid, turned crest rail that is tenoned and screwed to the posts. The screws are concealed by the carved sunflowers that cap the rails at the top of the posts. A series of five

internal plywood frames support both the laminated, veneered panel on the outside of the headboard and the rosewood tambours on the inside, in much the same way an airplane wing is fabricated. Both the headboard and footboard units bolt onto the side rails with threaded rods and captured nuts. Tongue-and-groove joints, as well as brass alignment pins and bushings, ensure the proper positioning of the units on the rails.

Using 1/8-in.-thick plywood patterns made from my full-scale drawings, I marked and cut the 3/4-in.-thick lumbercore plywood for the post core. I epoxied two layers of plywood to form a 1 1/2-in.-thick core and covered the edges with a prebent three-ply lamination of 3/8-in.-thick by 1 1/2-in.-wide mahogany to provide stability for the surface veneer. Next, I covered all the showing surfaces and edges with a highly figured makore veneer. I had found this veneer in New York City many years prior and had been saving it for a special occasion.

In spite of the richly figured makore, the bedposts still lacked definition. For this reason, I added the guitar-like endgrain mahogany edge trim that follows each curved edge. This detail terminates

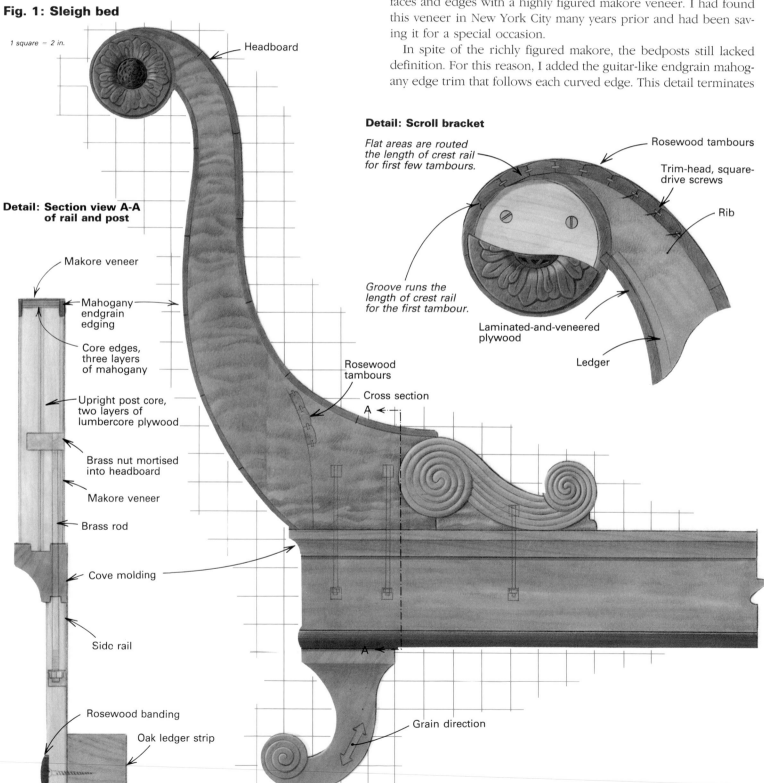

Fig. 1: Sleigh bed

1 square = 2 in.

Headboard

Detail: Scroll bracket

Flat areas are routed the length of crest rail for first few tambours.

Rosewood tambours

Trim-head, square-drive screws

Rib

Groove runs the length of crest rail for the first tambour.

Laminated-and-veneered plywood

Ledger

Detail: Section view A-A of rail and post

Makore veneer

Mahogany endgrain edging

Core edges, three layers of mahogany

Upright post core, two layers of lumbercore plywood

Brass nut mortised into headboard

Makore veneer

Brass rod

Rosewood tambours

Cross section

A

Cove molding

Side rail

Rosewood banding

Oak ledger strip

Grain direction

A

in a 360° turn, outlining the endgrain sunflower carving, which is shown in the photo on p. 23. I cut and inlaid the ⅛-in.-thick pieces of endgrain mahogany into rabbets. I routed along the edges of the post, as detailed in the sidebar on p. 27. Using endgrain mahogany to outline the posts also offered the structural advantage of easing the hard corners and protecting an otherwise vulnerable veneer joint.

The endgrain edging also creates a visual flow to other key elements of the headboard: The carved transitional scroll brackets at the base of the upright posts. The outside faces of these ⁸⁄₄ mahogany brackets were carved in dual, reversing spiral patterns, which provide visual relief from the posts' flat surfaces. To make the spiral design stand out, I veneered the field of the brackets with makore matched to the posts. The brackets were glued with polyvinyl acrylate (PVA) to the post core with a pair of ⅛-in.-thick Baltic-birch-plywood splines, as shown in figure 2 on the following page. Shopmade fasteners, similar to the mitered rail bolts, secure the headboard to the rails, and a tongue on the bottom of the brackets ensures proper alignment with the rails.

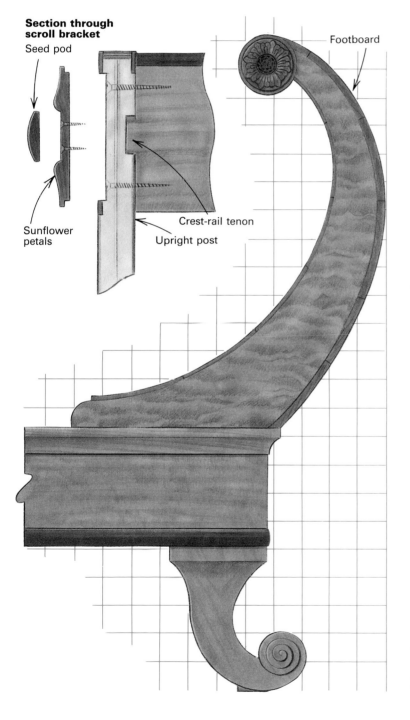

Section through scroll bracket

Seed pod

Sunflower petals

Crest-rail tenon

Upright post

Footboard

Slow-turning the large crest rail and assembling the internal framework

After the upright posts were completed and bolted into position, I turned the 6-in.-dia. solid-mahogany crest rail. (The footboard crest rail is 4 in. in diameter.) The size of the crest rail proved too taxing for my lathe, even running at its slowest speed, so I used a variable-speed portable drill to turn the crest-rail blank in the lathe at about 60 RPM. Then I built a jig to support and guide my router parallel to the axis of the lathe and used a ¾-in.-dia. fluting bit to do the cutting work. I turned the basic profile for the sunflower carvings before parting off these endgrain blanks. Next, I turned tenons on the ends of the crest rail that fit mortises drilled into the inside faces of the upright posts. The crest rail was then fit to the posts, and four, 3-in.-long sheet-metal screws were fastened through them and into the endgrain of the crest rail, as shown in figure 1 at left. (I didn't glue this joint in case the headboard ever needs to be disassembled.) To prepare the crest rail to accept the rosewood tambours, I routed flats and a groove in the rail, as shown in the detail in figure 1, to serve as an inset for the tambours and to provide a smooth and flowing transition from one surface to the other. I also routed a slot for the veneered outer panel.

The show surfaces of the headboard are supported by five internal frames, consisting of a ¾-in.-thick plywood rib and a ledger laminated from three layers of ⅛-in.-thick plywood. The frames are spaced evenly across the width of the headboard and span from the crest rail to the top of the end rail. Again, I used patterns taken from my full-scale drawings to lay out and cut the five ribs. The ledgers were then glued and screwed to the rib's edge to form the frames. The two outer frames were screwed to the inside face of the upright post, while the other frames were positioned and then screwed into the bottom of the crest rail. Although the bottoms of the frames are not secured at this time, once the outer face panel and the inner rosewood tambours are screwed in place, the entire structure becomes extremely rigid.

Rosewood tambours, curved laminated panels and some easier alternatives

With the framework complete, the next steps were to form the curved veneered panel for the outer face of the headboard and to apply the rosewood tambours on its inner face.

Bending, laminating and veneering the panel was a complicated and involved procedure that required gluing together three layers of ⅛-in.-thick plywood clamped between a male and a female form to shape the panel to the appropriate curve. As a way to avoid this process and simplify the construction, I recommend the same straightforward technique that I used on the inner face of the headboard to apply the rosewood tambours; this procedure—screwing through a tongue on each tambour into the ribs of the internal frame—is much the same as installing tongue-and-groove flooring. You might also try sliding canvas-backed tambour panels into grooves routed into the upright posts, in the same manner that tambour roll-top desks are made. However, the fit between the tambours won't be nearly as good as the method I used due to the changing radii of the various curves.

As a way of highlighting the rosewood tambours inside, I chose a smooth veneered panel for the outer surfaces of the headboard and footboard. I glued up these core panels with phenolic resin adhesive because of its extended drying time. The cores were shaped by clamping the laminates (three pieces of ⅛-in.-thick plywood) in the vacuum bag between a two-part form. This gave the panels the necessary curvature, which was shaped using spring poles off the ceiling of my shop. Once the cores were pressed into their corresponding shapes between the two forms, the vacuum

Fig. 2: Construction details

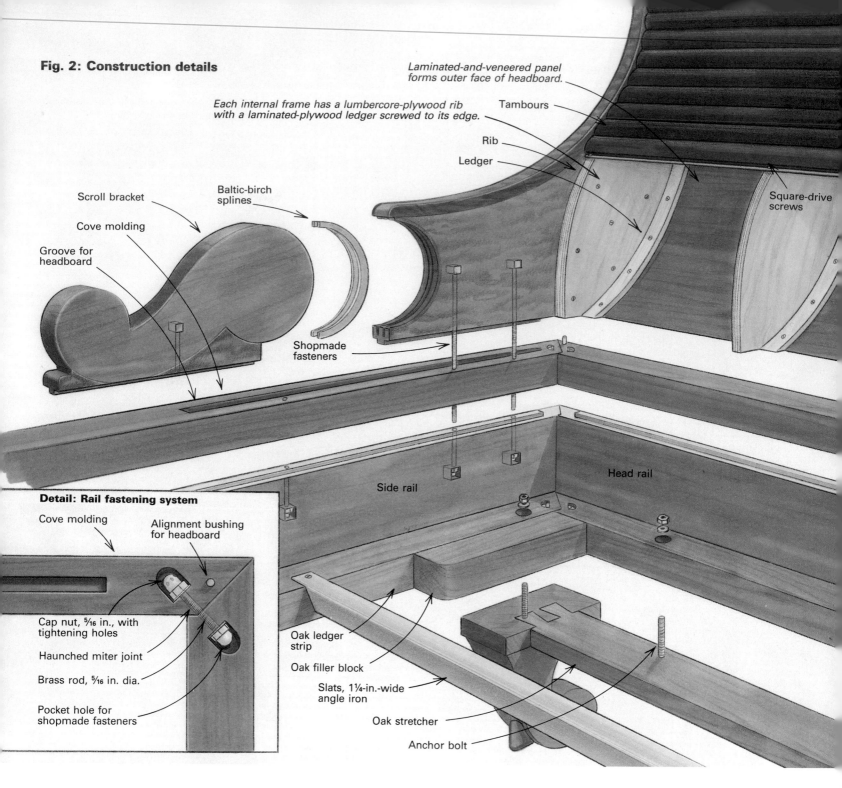

Each internal frame has a lumbercore-plywood rib with a laminated-plywood ledger screwed to its edge.

Laminated-and-veneered panel forms outer face of headboard.

Tambours

Rib

Ledger

Square-drive screws

Scroll bracket

Baltic-birch splines

Cove molding

Groove for headboard

Shopmade fasteners

Side rail

Head rail

Detail: Rail fastening system

Cove molding

Alignment bushing for headboard

Cap nut, ⁵⁄₁₆ in., with tightening holes

Haunched miter joint

Brass rod, ⁵⁄₁₆ in. dia.

Pocket hole for shopmade fasteners

Oak ledger strip

Oak filler block

Slats, 1¼-in.-wide angle iron

Oak stretcher

Anchor bolt

---

pump was turned on. Pressure was maintained throughout the approximately nine-hour set-up period. When the glued dried, the lamination was removed from the press, and the curved surfaces were scraped and faired. Although there was some springback, it proved manageable. Then I repeated the entire process to apply the fiddleback mahogany veneer to the core. After cutting and planing the finished panel so that it fit between the posts, I fit its top to the routed groove in the crest rail and its bottom flush to the head rail.

The rosewood tambours that I used on the inside surface of the headboard are made up of ⅝-in.-thick by 1¼-in.-wide strips, each lightly radiused, scraped and finish-sanded to 600-grit. Fitting and fastening these tambours was the last major procedure in making the headboard. I used splines instead of standard tongue-and-groove joints to allow me to plane both edges of the tambours for a precise fit and to conserve the precious rosewood. I first jointed the approximate edge angle needed for each tambour and then

fine-tuned the fit with a bench plane. A ¹⁄₁₆-in. gap between tambours accommodates normal wood movement. After fitting each tambour, I grooved its edges with a slot cutter on my router table.

To install the tambours, I assembled and leveled the bed rails on sawhorses, and then attached the headboard and footboard units. The first tambour, which fit into the recess routed in the crest rail, has a groove in one edge and a lap joint along the other edge that fits the crest rail's routed groove. I epoxied a spline into the groove of this first tambour, forming a tongue, and then predrilled for and fastened "trim-head," square-drive screws through this tongue and into the internal frames. All subsequent tambours were grooved on both edges. The groove on the top edge slipped onto the tongue of the preceding tambour, and, working from the top down, each tambour was in turn fastened to the internal frames through the tongue formed by a spline epoxied into the bottom groove. The tambours continue down below the level of the mattress and terminate just above the head rail.

Final touches: carved sunflowers and preparation for finishing

The final details of the headboard were the carved sunflowers that fit into the recesses at the top of the upright posts. The petals were first carved in the endgrain blanks parted from the ends of the mahogany crest rails. Next, the carved blanks were mounted into their recesses with screws that were in turn concealed by chip-carved rosewood seed pods that fit into mortises in the center of the sunflower carvings. To carve the seed pod, I photocopied the pattern and then glued copies to preturned and fitted blanks with spray-on contact adhesive. Paper patterns not only save time when carving multiples, but also eliminate trying to see pencil lines drawn on dark woods, like the rosewood. By turning the seed pods with slightly tapered sides, I could press-fit and spot-glue them into the recesses in the centers of the sunflowers. This way, I

could pry out the seed pods to gain access to the screws for disassembling or repairing the headboard if necessary.

I used different techniques to prepare the various materials of the bed for finishing. I sealed the veneered surfaces with a washcoat of 1½-lb. cut shellac before sanding, working up to a final sanding with 600-grit. I sanded the rosewood to 600-grit and buffed it with a soft brush to draw out the natural oils and give it luster. All the other surfaces were wet-sanded to 600-grit. I finished the bed with eight coats of Livos Kaldet oil, a non-toxic, citrus-base oil finish. (Livos Kaldet oil is available from The Natural Choice, 1365 Rufina Circle, Santa Fe, N.M. 87501; 505-438-3448.) Each coat was applied with a soft cloth, allowed to sit for up to two hours and then wiped dry. I lightly rubbed down each coat with 0000 steel wool. □

William Turner is a professional woodworker in Stonington, Maine.

A *vacuum fence for a tablesaw*

Inlaying endgrain mahogany edging on my sleigh bed required a special set of patterns and templates and many hours of tedious fitting, gluing and trimming. Between the headboard and the footboard, four different curves received this edge treatment, with each respective curve being repeated four times in order to inlay both the inside and outside edges of each post.

The 0.128-in.-thick pieces of inlay were cut from a 2-in.-long piece of mahogany that was 1¼ in. thick by 6 in. wide. To overcome the hazards of crosscutting such thin pieces from a small block, I developed a vacuum fence, shown in the drawing below, that is screwed to a sliding table for my tablesaw. Suction from an ordinary home vacuum cleaner, which connects to the back side of the fence, holds the blank in position on the face of the fence. I also notched the fence, as shown in the drawing, to counteract the upward and backward thrust of the blade. I had to turn the piece over and make a second pass due to the loss of blade height resulting from the ¾-in.-thick sliding table. Because the thin cutoff

is held securely to the fence, the piece won't be thrown back by the blade, and the cutoff won't vibrate against the blade, thus reducing sawmarks. This process yielded a high degree of accuracy and a consistent thickness, as well as minimal waste.

Rather than fitting four different sets of endgrain blocks for each curve, I saved time by first individually hand-fitting the 2-in.-long blocks side by side, to follow each curve of the upright posts. For each of the post's curves, I made up a ⅛-in.-thick plywood template that matched the shape of the upright post ½ in. from its edge. After mitering the edges of the blocks so that they butted together tightly and followed the edge of the pattern, I used spray adhesive to tack the blocks temporarily to the pattern. A ball-bearing-guided flush-trimming bit chucked in my router and run against the pattern trimmed the blanks to match the inner radii of each post's curves.

With the blocks shaped to the curve of the posts, I could then slice off the 0.128-in.-thick pieces, using my vacuum-fence setup, to form the endgrain inlay. I cut five

sets of inlays, making an extra set in case a piece was broken in the subsequent operations. I repeated this process to make endgrain inlay sets for the bed's four basic curves, storing the sets in separate parts bins to avoid confusion.

Then, with a ball-bearing-guided rabbeting bit, I routed ½-in.-wide by ⅛-in.-deep rabbets into the corners of the upright posts for the endgrain inlay. After making final adjustments to the fit with a file and plane, I glued, taped and clamped each piece of inlay into its rabbet. When the glue dried, the clamps were removed, and with the bearing-guided flush-trimming bit, I routed the endgrain inlay even to the edge of the posts. Next, I carefully leveled the inlay, which was 0.003 in. proud of the posts, with a mill file and then lightly radiused the corners. Duct tape wrapped around the end of the file helped protect the 1/64-in.-thick makore veneer on the face of the posts. Although the process was long and involved, the effect was exactly what I wanted: The major curves of the bed were outlined and defined. —*W.T.*

Fig. 3: Vacuum fence

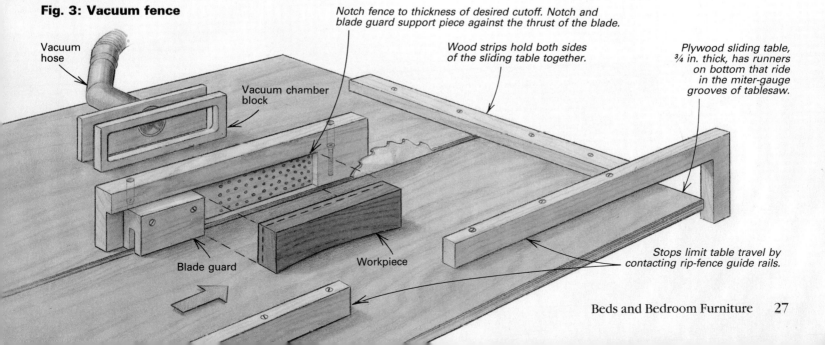

Notch fence to thickness of desired cutoff. Notch and blade guard support piece against the thrust of the blade.

Vacuum hose

Vacuum chamber block

Wood strips hold both sides of the sliding table together.

Plywood sliding table, ¾ in. thick, has runners on bottom that ride in the miter-gauge grooves of tablesaw.

Blade guard

Workpiece

Stops limit table travel by contacting rip-fence guide rails.

Bending a Big Curve
Laminations with spindles make this bed a Windsor

by Jeff Miller

Like the familiar chairs from which it gets its name, this Windsor bed, with its laminated curves and simple spindles, looks equally at home in either a rustic or a contemporary setting.

W hen the idea for making a Windsor bed first came to mind, the basic form was obvious—classic and simple—but the details of construction most certainly were not. The first bed was a learning experience, and each subsequent version has improved execution. The key process is laminating the bent arches that define the headboard and footboard, and after building a hundred or so, we've solved most of the real problems.

The basic technique is to layer up a plywood form with fitted cauls for each bend, so you can clamp many thin layers of wood into the shape you want. This technique will work in any situation where you want a wooden curve, at virtually any scale. We've used it to develop a full line of beds as well as components in chairs, tables and other pieces of furniture.

There are a few tools you can't do without when working with bent laminations. First you will need a lot of clamps: a minimum of twelve 2-ft.-long bar clamps per bending (more is better here) and two 6-ft.-long bar or pipe clamps to span the full width of each bending. And second, I've found a jointer and planer indispensable for cleaning up the rough bendings. I suppose it's possible to do this some other way—but I'm not sure I'd have the fortitude.

Making the laminations

You can rip the many laminates you need from solid stock, or you can buy thick veneer and cut it up. For the queen-size Windsor bed, you need 34 strips of wood, each roughly ¹⁄₁₀ in. thick, 2¼ in. wide

and 10 ft. long, as shown in the drawing on p. 31. Our Windsor bed is made of cherry, but most hard woods bend well, except oak, which tends to splinter. For the first Windsor bed, it took two of us the whole day to rip solid stock. We took frequent breaks for the motor on my 8-in. tablesaw to cool down, for resetting the tripped circuit breaker and for sweeping up the mess. After that, I swore off this method and ripped thick veneers for the next 70 beds. At first we ripped the veneer with a portable circular saw and a long straightedge, and then we found that the veneer was thick enough to cut on the tablesaw. Both methods are fairly messy, and a good portion of the expensive veneer was wasted (we used the waste on other projects, but much is unusable unless you need unlimited shims).

Eventually, we returned to ripping from solid stock with a more powerful saw, a better outfeed setup and dust collection. With our new setup, one person can do the whole job in a few hours. The results are better than the veneer method: tighter bendings and cleaner finished surfaces. After costing it out, we came out slightly ahead. Labor was higher, but material costs were lower.

To make these long rips of wood easier and safer to handle, mill the wood into manageable blanks; for the bed, make two 10-ft. blanks, 2¼ in. thick by 4½ in. wide. Mark layout triangles on the faces of the boards so that you can put the rippings back together in sequence. Then set your tablesaw fence so that a ¹⁄₁₀-in.-wide strip will be ripped off to the outside of the blade. Rip the two blanks, then reset the fence. If the blank starts to curve from the release of internal stress or if you burn or nick the edge by flinching when ripping, you'll have to joint the edge before continuing. Refer to your layout triangles to keep the strips in sequence as they come off the blanks. Do not try to rip those last couple of strips when the blank gets too narrow. It's much too dangerous.

Building bending forms

You will need two D-shaped bending forms: one for the headboard and one for the footboard, as shown in the drawing on p. 31. Each form is three layers of ¾-in. plywood, totaling 2¼ in. thick. You will need four sheets of plywood, and even this will require piecing scraps together. There are many ways to lay out an ellipse. I use a jig like the one described in *FWW* #86 (pp. 88-90) but with a pencil mounted on the bar instead of a router.

After laying out the form patterns on sheets of plywood, cut them out and sand them smooth. Then use these forms to mark out the other layers, piecing the middle layer together to save materials. Bandsaw slightly outside of the line, screw and glue the second and third layers to the faired form, and then flush-trim with a router and a bearing-guided bit.

Lay out the cauls by marking a line 1¾ in. outside the forms. To do this, make a 3½-in.-dia. disc from ¼-in. plywood, stick a pencil in the center hole and roll it around the edge of the form. The cauls for the curved sections are made in three pieces while straight 2x4s are adequate cauls for the straight sections.

After laying out the curved cauls, make a locating mark to line them up with the form. Once the cauls are bandsawn, smoothed and assembled, line up these marks and tack on guide strips (see the drawing). Mark the forms to show the bottom of the bendings, and then wax the forms, cauls and guide strips.

A methodical glue-up

Gluing up the bendings must be approached methodically. Everything must be ready and close at hand. It wouldn't hurt to do a dry run. The tighter curves of the footboard increase the difficulty, so start with the headboard.

We use Weldwood plastic resin glue for all bent laminations. The glue doesn't creep under tension and doesn't impart as much moisture to the wood as regular yellow glue. However, plastic resin, which is actually urea formaldehyde glue and which comes in powder form, does need to be handled with much more care. Wear a mask to avoid breathing the powder, and wear gloves and goggles to prevent contact with the mixed glue.

Spread out a bundle of strips on the cleanly swept floor, and set one strip (the top piece) a little apart from the other 16 strips to avoid spreading glue on it. Set the form on the floor (or on a large worktable) nearby, with cauls and clamps at hand. We've found that 1,000cc of glue powder and 400cc of water is about right for one bending. It is fairly difficult to stir all the lumps out, so we use a paint mixer in an electric drill. Spread the glue evenly over one side of the 16 strips, not both, with a short-nap paint roller. Then bundle them back up in order (don't forget to add the top strip), and lay the bundle at the top of the form. The clamping pressure will transfer the glue to the mating surfaces.

Start clamping from the center and work toward both ends, placing clamps alternately to the top and the bottom. Working around the sharp bends is most difficult because the clamps get in the way of each other. Sometimes you can use a block of wood as a spacer between the clamp and the caul to get some of the excess clamp outside the clutter (see the photo above). Leave the bendings to set overnight. If your shop will be cooler than 65°, you should cover the assembly with an electric blanket.

Apply clamps beginning at the center of the curve, and then work in both directions. An occasional block inserted between clamp and caul helps keep the clamp handles from interfering with one another. Guide strips screwed to the form interlock with similar strips on the cauls.

Before the bendings come out of the forms, mark the finished lengths on them. After removing the bendings, transfer your marks to the inside faces where they won't get planed off, and trim the bendings a couple of inches long for now. Running these unwieldy things over the jointer seems harder than it is. Placing supports at both ends will make the process easier, as will an assistant. A wider jointer is a help. Keep as much of the bending as possible over the jointer table at all times.

Thickness planing is probably the strangest looking procedure in the whole project, though it is actually straightforward and a lot of fun. You just steer the bending through the planer, as shown in the top photo on the following page, watching to make sure it doesn't bind on its way around the curve. Plane to 1¾ in., then cut the bendings to final length. Scrape and sand the outsides and insides, and beltsand the fronts and backs.

Joining rails and spindles to the bendings

Most projects involving bent laminations will require some additional edge-shaping, which you should leave until after you cut the joints. On our Windsor bed, through-mortises and wedged tenons join the rails to the bendings. We cut these joints with a plunge router and some simple templates. The mortise is a little easier to rout if you begin by drilling a few holes straight through the bending with the template clamped in place.

Before cutting the headboard and footboard rails to length, mark the face of the bending to show where the inside face of the side rails will fall. The measurement between side rails should be ¼ in. more than the width of the mattress to allow room for bedding. So make sure the tenon shoulders on the headboard and footboard rails will give you that dimension (59⁹⁄₁₆ in. for standard queen size). And don't forget to add length for the through-tenons before you crosscut the rails. Cut the side rails to length at the same time. For most queen- and king-size mattresses, 81 in. will allow a little room for tucking in the bedding and wiggling the toes.

The Windsor bed has 40 spindles totaling 90 lineal feet of dowel, which I would advise against trying to make from scratch. I made the dowels with a router jig for my first Windsor bed. It was a lot of work and the resulting spindles required much sanding and fussing. I've bought my dowel stock ever since. Midwest Dowel Works (4631 Hutchinson Road, Cincinnati, Ohio 45248;

Assembling the headboard and footboard

With all the joints done, round over the edges of the bendings with a ¼-in.-radius router bit, and chamfer the edges of the rails. Cut sawkerfs in the tenons for the wedges that will be hammered in later, and cut the wedges from a contrasting wood. To determine the lengths of the outer three footboard spindles, which are inserted now, place the rail on the bending where it will be when installed, and measure from the bottom of the holes to about 1 in. below the bending. Make certain these spindles will fit in the holes—we drill up a test block—and insert them without glue.

Glue-up is fairly simple. Spread glue in the mortises, and very lightly on the rail tenons, slip one end in, and spring the bending to slip the other in. Two long clamps located above and below the joints are all that you need. Spread glue on the wedges and tap them home.

Now measure for the rest of the spindles, this time from the bottom of the holes in the rails to just below the bending at the corresponding hole. Cut spindles to length and number them. Then check for fit in your test block, and sand for fit and finish. With one hand near the bottom end of the spindle and the other near its middle, flex the spindle enough to insert it (without glue) into the proper hole. When it bottoms out, the spindle should just fit under its hole in the bending.

By now, the glue on the rail joints should be set, and the clamps can come off. The wedges need to be trimmed off and sanded flush. Then clamp the assembled headboard or footboard upside down in a bench vise. Spread a little glue in each spindle hole in the bending, and push the spindles all the way into the holes. Complete the spindling process by tacking ⅝-in.-long brads through the spindles from the inside of the rail.

Attaching side rails and cleats

There are numerous methods for attaching bed rails to a headboard and footboard. All manner of hardware options exist that claim to provide easy assembly and disassembly and a solid joint. I prefer the rock solid feel of bolts (either actual bed bolts or ⁵⁄₁₆-in. by 5½-in. hex head bolts with washers), which are only slightly less convenient than instant, knockdown hardware. With bolts, there is no screwing into endgrain and so no worry that something will work loose. The key to this joint is a recess for the nut routed on the inside of the rail about 3¼ in. from each end of the rails. The recess could be large enough for an open-end wrench, but we prefer to allow just enough room for a screwdriver to be inserted alongside a flat on the nut to wedge it from turning. A wrench seems to encourage excessive tightening.

Two dowels in the side rail ends, one on either side of the bolt hole, provide additional strength, prevent the rail from twisting and help with alignment when assembling the bed. We finish the joint by counterboring the outside of the bolt holes, so the head of the bolt and a washer will seat below the surface. You can conceal the hardware with a plug if you want.

The bed is now ready for finishing. We usually finish with three coats of Watco Danish oil, rubbed on with progressively finer grit sandpaper (220, 320, 400) followed by a final coat of wax. After the rails are completely finished, you can screw on the cleats, set up the frame and measure the exact length of the slats.

We use 16 crosswise slats, ¾ in. thick by 4 in. wide, with their edges rounded over and their ends located by ⁵⁄₁₆-in. dowel pins in the cleats, which fit notches in the ends of the slats. For a king-size bed, add a center strut from headboard to footboard. Drop the slats into place, and step back to admire your handiwork. ☐

Jeff Miller builds custom furniture in Chicago.

The author guides the unwieldy bending through his planer (after jointing one face flat) to true up the other face and to mill the curved piece to the proper thickness.

Miller uses a shopmade square to align the spindle holes in the curved parts. He also uses the wooden square to transfer the hole locations from the rail (which he temporarily clamps in place) to the curve. To start holes on the steep part of a curve, he uses a drill bit with a long center pilot.

513-574-8488) carries a wide range of quality hardwood dowels.

It is very difficult to assemble the spindles when you glue the rail to the bending, so you insert them afterward. The trick is to drill deeper into the rail than into the bending to provide clearance and then to shove the spindles up into the bending and glue them tight.

Mark out 20 centers on the headboard and footboard rails 2¾ in. apart. Dry-assemble the rails with the bendings: insert one tenon into its mortise most of the way, and then spring the bending open enough to slip the other tenon in. With a large, shopmade square, transfer the marks onto the bendings. Remove the rails, and use the drill press to bore ⅝-in.-dia. holes, 2 in. deep, along the top edge of each rail. Drill the three outer holes on each side of the footboard rail 1 in. deeper. This will allow you to insert those spindles while gluing up the bendings with the rails, because they are quite difficult to install afterward.

The holes in the bendings have to be parallel to the straight legs, so clamp the part upside down in a bench vise with the legs perpendicular to the bench surface, as shown in the bottom photo above. Sight down a square resting on the bench surface to help drill straight, and then wrap a piece of tape around the drill bit as a depth indicator. You need a bit with a long pilot (we use a Powerbore bit) for drilling on the steep angles of the bend. On the two outermost holes on the headboard bending, you may have to start the bit at an angle, and you will probably have to fuss these holes with a small gouge or rasp. Check the alignment of these holes now—they're much harder to fiddle with later.

From *Fine Woodworking* (January 1993) 98:70-73

Bed basics

Standard mattress sizes are given in the chart below, but when building a bed, always measure the actual mattress to be used because industry standards can vary greatly. Don't forget to measure the thickness of the mattress (a concern that may not be immediately obvious). The measurements that are given in the drawing are for a queen-size bed with a 7-in.-thick mattress used without a box spring. For a box spring and mattress, use wider rails and increase the length of the straight part of the bendings to avoid having the mattress extend up over the bend in the footboard.

On our beds, we use cleats on all four rails to support a box spring and add 16 slats to create a platform for futons or mattresses without a box spring. To locate the slats and to keep them from sliding around (and to keep the mattress and you from falling through), we insert dowels along the side rail cleats (see the drawing detail). —J.M.

Standard mattresses

Twin	39 x 75
Double (full)	54 x 75
Queen	60 x 80
King	76 x 80

Detail: Side rails

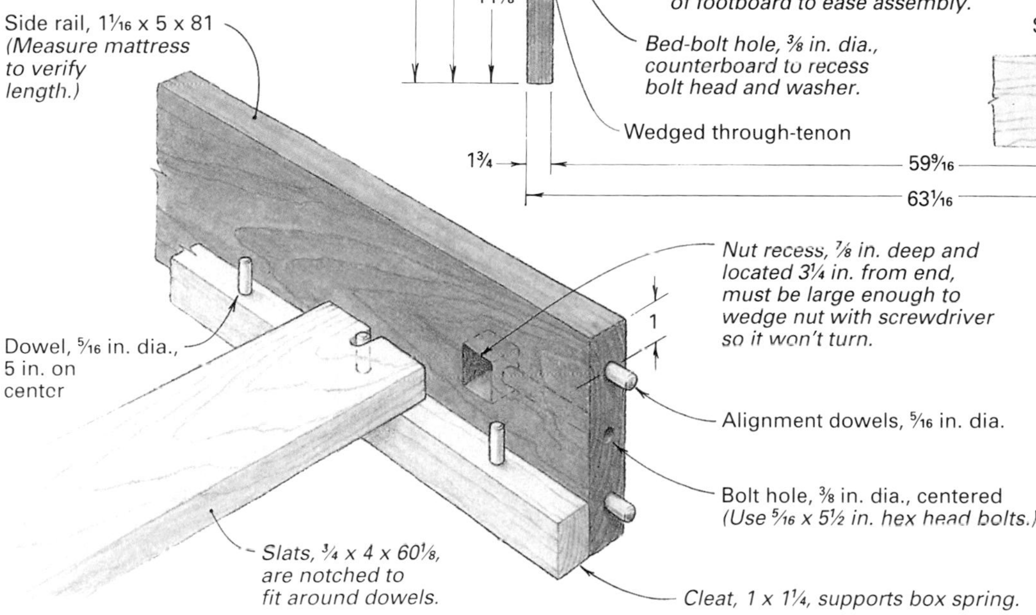

Side rail, 1¹⁄₁₆ x 5 x 81 (Measure mattress to verify length.)

Dowel, ⁵⁄₁₆ in. dia., 5 in. on center

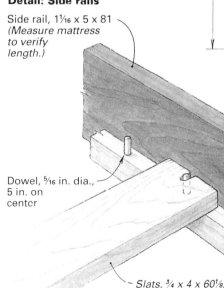

Slats, ¼ x 4 x 60⅛, are notched to fit around dowels.

Nut recess, ⅞ in. deep and located 3¼ in. from end, must be large enough to wedge nut with screwdriver so it won't turn.

Alignment dowels, ⁵⁄₁₆ in. dia.

Bolt hole, ⅜ in. dia., centered (Use ⁵⁄₁₆ x 5½ in. hex head bolts.)

Cleat, 1 x 1¼, supports box spring.

Headboard and footboard for a Windsor bed

Curves of headboard and footboard are based on ellipses. Drawings show finished bed on left, bending form on right.

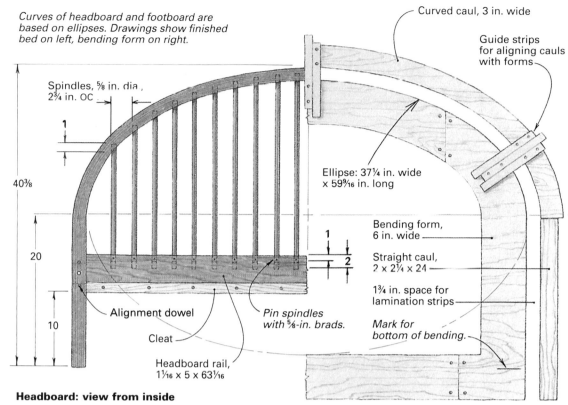

Spindles, ⅝ in. dia., 2¾ in. OC

40⅜

20

10

Alignment dowel

Cleat

Headboard rail, 1¹⁄₁₆ x 5 x 63¹⁄₁₆

Pin spindles with ⅝-in. brads.

Curved caul, 3 in. wide

Guide strips for aligning cauls with forms

Ellipse: 37¼ in. wide x 59⁹⁄₁₆ in. long

Bending form, 6 in. wide

Straight caul, 2 x 2¼ x 24

1¾ in. space for lamination strips

Mark for bottom of bending.

Note: Bending forms and curved caul sections are 2¼ in. thick, pieced together from three layers of ¾-in. plywood.

Headboard: view from inside

Laminated curves are 17 strips, ¹⁄₁₀ in. thick by 2¼ in. wide. After gluing, plane to about 1¾ in. thick. Finished width can vary depending on thickness of laminae.

Footboard: view from outside

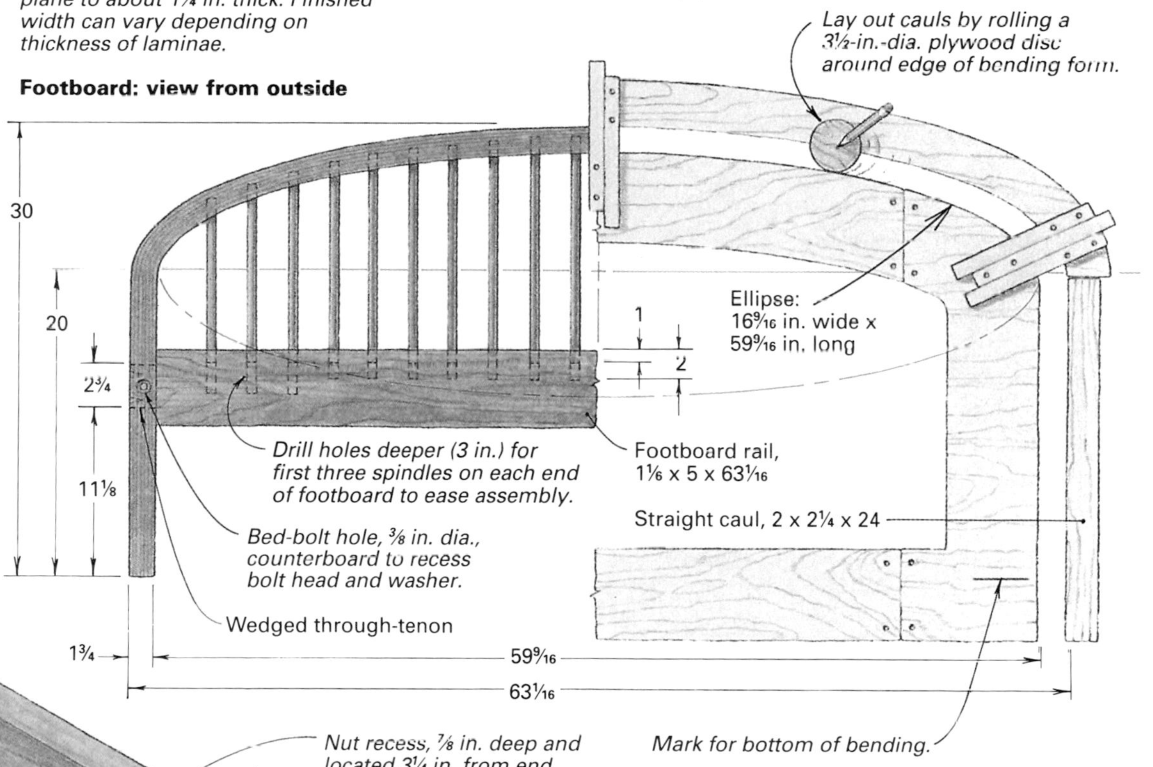

Lay out cauls by rolling a 3½-in.-dia. plywood disc around edge of bending form.

30

20

2¾

11⅛

1¾

Drill holes deeper (3 in.) for first three spindles on each end of footboard to ease assembly.

Bed-bolt hole, ⅜ in. dia., counterbored to recess bolt head and washer.

Wedged through-tenon

Footboard rail, 1¹⁄₁₆ x 5 x 63¹⁄₁₆

Straight caul, 2 x 2¼ x 24

Ellipse: 16⁹⁄₁₆ in. wide x 59⁹⁄₁₆ in. long

59⁹⁄₁₆

63¹⁄₁₆

Mark for bottom of bending.

Note: Length of rails will have to be adjusted if lamination is not exactly 1¾ in. wide. Measurement between side rails should be ¼ in. more than width of mattress. Overall height should be adjusted for mattress thickness. Dimensions are for a standard queen size mattress.

With safety and practicality in mind, Brad Rubin built this crib, striving for a contemporary look and hidden hardware. He drew components with his personal computer and then fashioned his own drop-side mechanisms. The resulting crib in oiled maple is simple, easy to clean and easy to use. Two-year-old son Justin, ready for his morning nap, agrees.

Crib Hides Its Hardware

Commercial drawer slides are the key

by Bradley S. Rubin

From *Fine Woodworking* (May 1993) 100:72-75

While waiting for your baby to be born, a crib is the best piece of furniture you can make. Cribmaking offers quite a few woodworking challenges and can help you burn off nervous energy. Building a crib is more practical than making a cradle because a baby can sleep in a crib every day for several years, but a cradle is only useful for about as many months.

When I designed the crib shown in the photo on the facing page, I had several goals in mind. First, the crib had to be safe. That meant it had to be sturdy, and it had to comply with standard safety regulations. Second, I didn't want unsightly metal hardware exposed when the crib's drop side was up. Third, I wanted the crib to have a contemporary look rather than appear traditional with turned spindles, like those commonly found in furniture stores. Finally, I wanted the crib to be collapsible for easy moving and storage and to have a drop side that would operate smoothly.

Because safety was the most crucial constraint, I designed the crib around eight of the regulations that the United States Consumer Product Safety Commission publishes (see the crib safety box on p. 34). I drew up an initial plan using my personal computer and a computer-aided drafting package. The drawing software (Generic CADD) lets me modify things repeatedly, so I could see resulting proportions, take measurements for a cutting list and make sure that the mattress and support spring would fit.

Selecting wood and bedding

I decided the crib should be made of a durable wood and have a nontoxic finish. I chose hard maple for all the components, partly because it's plentiful in Minnesota. But my chief reasons for using maple are that it's attractive and that once it's sanded and oiled, its close-grained texture makes it easy to clean. I was even fortunate enough to find wood with bird's-eye figure for the posts. Next, my wife, Debbie, and I picked out a crib mattress and a spring to support it. Although most cribs have adjustable-height mattresses, I decided to keep things simple by fixing the mattress height. I made the crib's mattress-to-rail height 22 in.

Choosing drop-side hardware and accessories

It's essential that a crib have a drop side. For one thing, it makes lifting a child in and out of the crib much easier on your back. Another reason is it gives you better access to change the baby's sheets. Finally, when a crib's side is lowered, it gives you one other convenient place to change the baby's diapers—something you need to do much more often than I suspected.

Most cribs have two drop sides, but I made this crib with just one movable side. Because the crib's ends are the same, the crib can

To drop the side, the author adapted standard drawer slides. A pair of spring-loaded pins, one on each end of the crib, latch the side in its up position.

be placed either way, so the drop side faces into a room. While many suppliers carry drop-side hardware (see the sources of supply box on p. 35), I was unable to find the concealed system I had in mind. So I fashioned my own mechanisms by slightly modifying standard hardware items (see the photo below).

Adapting a pair of drawer slides—After looking through a few woodworking supply catalogs, I realized that a pair of heavy-duty drawer slides (the ones used in file cabinets) would be sturdy and would provide enough travel (11 in.) to lower and raise the crib's side. The drawer slides I chose (see the sources of supply box) move precisely and smoothly because they have a ball-bearing carriage that runs between two tracks. But the best part about the slides is that their thin profile lets me recess them into the crib's drop side and posts, thus keeping the workings out of sight.

Making a latch mechanism—I made two latches (spring-loaded pull pins) that take an adult's arm span to disengage at the same time and that take an adult's strength to unlatch (to overcome the pins' spring force). Each latch has a slightly undersized ¼-in. dowel, a spring, a washer and a cotter pin that retains the spring on the dowel. The dowels engage holes drilled in the posts. For pulls, I glued round wooden knobs to the dowel ends, as shown in the drawing detail on p. 35. If I had to make the latches over again, I'd probably peg the pulls to the dowels in addition to gluing them.

Other hardware—While I was buying hardware for the drop side, I also picked up a few other necessities for the crib, including four 2-in.-dia. casters designed to roll easily on carpeting and two plastic teething rails. In addition, I bought four sets of metal bed-rail fasteners to attach the crib's fixed side to the ends. The fasteners let me quickly knock the crib down into four pieces.

Crib construction

The drawing on pp. 34-35 shows how the mattress spring rests on two lengthwise stretchers. Mortises in the mid rails of the crib ends support the stretchers. Screws driven from below the stretcher ends into the mid rails keep the crib framework rigid and allow for easy disassembly.

The vertical slats (bars) for the crib's ends and sides measure 1 in. by ½ in. and have ⅛-in.-radius rounded edges. All the slat ends are drilled for ¼-in. dowels. I used spiral-grooved dowels, so the rail-to-slat joints would be secure; once these dowels are glued, the slats aren't likely to twist. Working all the slats into mating dowel holes and getting the faces of the slats parallel to the

Corner construction

Through dovetail

Pros: Very strong, great mechanical strength and large long-grain to long-grain glue area. The hand-cut through dovetail is aesthetically strong, too. End grain shows on the drawer face, providing a pleasing contrast in some furniture styles.

Cons: The end grain exposed on the face may be inappropriate on more traditionally styled pieces. Comparatively speaking, the dovetail is a time-consuming joint to cut, and it takes practice before you can cut it well. Router jigs used to make through dovetails are relatively expensive, and the resulting joint can look too uniform.

Half-blind dovetail

Pros: As with the through dovetail, half-blind dovetails are very strong and look great, too. And because the joint doesn't show on the drawer face, it's ideal for even the most formal and traditional drawers.

Cons: Even more time-consuming and finnicky to cut by hand than through dovetails. Routed half-blind dovetails look routed because of the minimum width of the pins. Most jigs don't allow flexible spacing of pins and tails.

Rabbeted half dovetail

Pros: Simple to cut (one pass on the router table for each drawer component), simple to clamp and quite handsome. When pinned with dowels, it's a mechanically strong joint.

Cons: Not as strong as through- or half-blind dovetails and without the traditional cachet. All glue-surface area is end grain to long grain, a weaker connection than long grain to long grain.

Sliding dovetail

Pros: Very strong, easy to cut once set up. Can be made so the joint is visible at the top edge of the drawer or so the joint is hidden (stopped).

Cons: Difficult to fit and assemble. The fit should be a bit loose when the joint is dry because glue will start to bind the joint almost immediately. You'll need to work fast once you've applied the glue.

Blind-dado rabbet

Pros: Good production joint. It's quick to cut on the router table once it's set up. With a dedicated bit, setup is quick, too. Joint is hidden from front and looks nice if done well.

Cons: Time-consuming to set up unless you have a dedicated bit, which is expensive. Only fair mechanical strength and all glue-surface area is end grain to long grain. Side edges of drawer front are vulnerable to chipping if they're not beveled slightly.

shared by the two joined parts or by the way the parts interlock mechanically.

Dovetails make the strongest joints— In a chest of drawers, most any well-made joint will be strong enough because the weight the drawers will have to bear is minimal. But stuff a drawer with reams of paper, a dozen handplanes or a blender, assorted bowls and a Cuisinart, and you've upped the ante.

In situations where I know a drawer is going to have to stand up to some heavy use, I like to use a dovetail joint. Through, half-blind and sliding dovetails (see the photos at left) will stand up to almost any use or abuse imaginable. Short of destroying a drawer, you're not likely to see a well-made dovetail joint fail. So choosing one of these three joints becomes a question of aesthetics and efficiency.

A simpler joint in the back— Often a drawer is held together with two kinds of joints: something a little fancier in the front where it will show and something simpler in the back where strength, not appearance, is the primary consideration. In the chest shown at left, I joined the backs of the top four drawers to the sides with sliding dovetails because they're strong, and I can make them quickly with a router.

There's one situation in which you can't use a sliding dovetail at the back of a drawer: when you want to capture a plywood drawer bottom on all four sides, as I did on the bottom drawer in this chest. For that drawer, I used dado-rabbet joints at the back corners. The dadoes run from top to bottom on the drawer sides, just in from the ends. The back is rabbeted to engage the dado and is flush with the back end of the sides.

Quartersawn lumber is best— Another functional consideration is stability: how much the drawer will move with seasonal changes in humidity. A drawer that's swollen shut is obviously useless, but one with a huge gap at the top isn't very attractive. So I try to use quartersawn lumber for the sides and backs of drawers whenever possible. It's much more dimensionally stable than flatsawn stock and less likely to warp or twist.

Regardless of whether I'm using quartersawn or flatsawn lumber, I make sure the drawer stock is thoroughly seasoned. I also try to let it acclimate in my shop for a few weeks before working it.

Choosing wood for sides, back, runners— For drawer sides and backs, I generally select a wood that's different from the fronts. Secondary wood saves a little money. And there's no need to waste really spectacular lumber on drawer sides or backs. I use a wood that moves about the same amount seasonally as the drawer fronts and is long-wearing. I also use this secondary wood for the drawer runners. This prevents the sides from wearing a groove in the runners or the runners from wearing down the sides.

Using a secondary wood for the sides of a drawer also can set up an interesting contrast when the drawer is opened, especially with a lighter-colored wood.

Aim for a thin drawer side— Drawer-side thickness is a concern for both structural and aesthetic reasons. What you're trying to achieve is a drawer that's light, strong and well-proportioned. For this chest, I used ⅜ in.-thick drawer sides for the top pair of drawers. I added ¹⁄₁₆ in. thickness to the sides and back of each descending drawer. Graduated drawers distinguish this piece from production work; each drawer has sufficient strength and pleasing proportions.

Aesthetics: Make it attractive and appropriate

The next consideration is appearance. A nailed rabbet joint, for example, may work perfectly well but just wouldn't make it in a reproduction American highboy. All of the joints I used in this chest of drawers are attractive, but some are more refined than others. So the choice of joinery, especially at the front of the drawer, may hinge on the expectations or tastes of the client and the style of the piece.

To my eye, the through dovetail, the half-blind dovetail and the rabbeted half dovetail work better aesthetically with this piece than do the sliding dovetail or blind-dado rabbet. But for drawers in a kitchen island or a child's bureau, I'd probably go with the sliding dovetail or the blind-dado rabbet because neither of these furniture pieces requires fancy joinery.

Efficiency: Can I make it quickly and easily?

Ease and speed of construction are related concerns, especially if you make your living as a furnituremaker. As a professional, I have to weigh the time it takes to cut and assemble a joint against what it adds to the piece. I also have to know whether the client is willing to pay for the extra labor. If you're an amateur woodworker, time probably is less of a concern, but there will still be projects you just want to finish.

The relative difficulty of making a particular joint also may be a consideration. If you've never cut dovetails by hand before, it's probably a good idea to practice before you start cutting into those figured-maple drawer fronts.

If you have no desire to cut dovetails by hand, a number of router jigs will cut dovetails that are just as strong or stronger than hand-cut ones. But with a few exceptions, they all give you dovetails that look rigidly uniform and machine-made. These may not be the right choice on a piece of furniture that traditionally would have had hand-cut dovetails. And even if routed dovetails work for you aesthetically, there's a learning curve for most of these jigs. So while there may be some gain in efficiency over time, you shouldn't plan to buy a jig on Saturday to speed you through your dovetails on Sunday.

A router can help you make other good-looking, simple joints that are plenty strong. The sliding dovetail and the blind-dado rabbet on the bottom two drawers of this chest fit the bill on all counts.

Supporting drawer bottoms

Corner joinery is only one facet of drawer construction. There's also the question of how to support the drawer bottom. What's wrong with a simple groove cut near the bottom of the drawer sides? Not a thing for most work (see the drawing at left on p. 42), but if you check out a really first-rate

> The object
> is to build
> a strong, stable,
> attractive drawer
> in a reasonable
> amount of time.

From *Fine Woodworking* (March 1996) 117:45-49

Bottom construction

Fully enclosed plywood panel

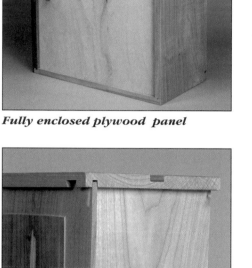

Solid raised panel in a groove

Plywood panel in a drawer slip

Rabbeted solid panel in a drawer slip

Mix and match: You can support a drawer bottom in grooves cut in the drawer sides or in slips glued to the sides. Drawer bottoms can be made of plywood or solid wood. Either material is compatible with either method of support. Your choice will be based on time, cost and the piece's function.

Grooves

Grooved drawer sides provide plenty of support for most drawer bottoms, as long as the drawers aren't going to carry a lot of weight. Sides should be sized proportionally to the width of the drawer.

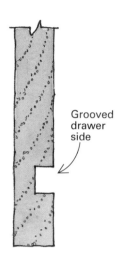

Grooved drawer side

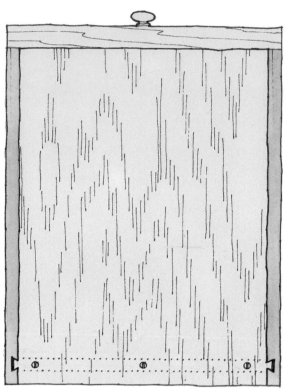

Plywood bottom A plywood bottom can be supported on three sides and screwed to the back of the drawer (above) or totally enclosed and supported in grooves on all four sides (top photo at left).

antique, chances are good that the drawer will be riding on slips (see the drawing at left on the facing page).

Drawer slips are strips of wood glued to the bottom inside faces of the drawer sides. They sit flush with the bottom of the side and are grooved to accept a drawer bottom. Designed to increase the running surface of the drawer, slips prevent the drawer side from wearing a groove in the runner. They also prevent a thin drawer side from being weakened by a groove. I used drawer slips on two of the drawers shown at left: one with a plywood bottom and one with a rabbeted, solid-cedar bottom.

Slips are more than just functional additions to a drawer. They add a measure of finish and formality that catches your eye. I didn't add any decorative elements to the slips in this drawer, but you could bead the

top inside edge of the slip, cove it or round it over to add more visual interest, as shown in the drawings above.

Plywood or solid wood?

The other big decision is whether to make the drawer bottoms from plywood or from solid wood.

Plywood is stronger but not traditional—Plywood has many advantages over solid wood, but for some purists, it is simply unacceptable.

Plywood is dimensionally stable, so you don't have to take wood movement into consideration. It is stronger for a given thickness than solid material, so you can use a thinner piece: 1/4-in. plywood is thick enough for a drawer bottom (I usually use a 1/2-in. panel if it's solid wood). This also

Slips

Drawer slips add strength and rigidity and increase the drawer's bearing surface on the runners. Slips can be simple, grooved pieces of wood, or they can be made more decorative, as shown at right.

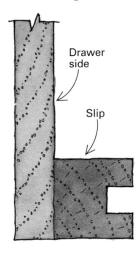

Drawer side

Slip

Slip profiles

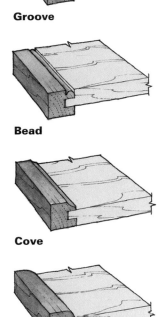

Groove

Bead

Cove

Half round

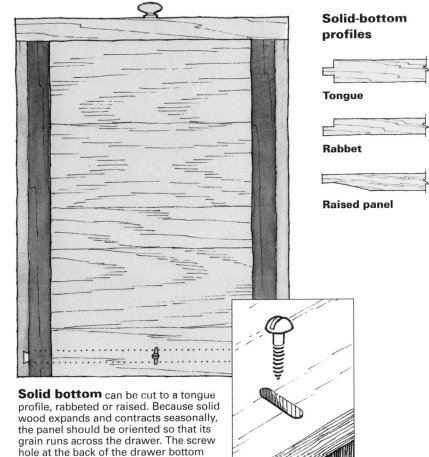

Solid-bottom profiles

Tongue

Rabbet

Raised panel

Solid bottom can be cut to a tongue profile, rabbeted or raised. Because solid wood expands and contracts seasonally, the panel should be oriented so that its grain runs across the drawer. The screw hole at the back of the drawer bottom should be elongated (right).

---

makes plywood a good choice if you're concerned with weight.

One problem with using plywood is that the actual thickness of a ¼-in. sheet is about ⁷⁄₃₂ in. That means that if you rout a ¼-in. groove in a slip or in your drawer sides, the plywood panel will flop around. Instead, I use a ³⁄₁₆-in. bit and make two passes. I get a perfect fit, but it takes more time. Of course, there are dado sets available that will plow a ⁷⁄₃₂-in. groove, but you can't always run the groove the length of the drawer piece. On some drawer fronts, for instance, you need a stopped groove.

Installing solid-wood bottoms—For solid wood drawer bottoms, the grain must run side to side in the drawer, rather than front to back, so wood expansion won't push the drawer apart and shrinkage won't

create a gap at the sides. I usually either rabbet or raise a panel on a solid-wood drawer bottom so the edge is thinner than the rest of the field (see the solid bottom profiles above). This lets me plow a smaller groove in the drawer sides. The result is a strong, sturdy panel that will not weaken the drawer slips or sides excessively.

A rabbeted panel can be slid in with the raised portion facing either up or down. When I use drawer slips and a rabbeted panel, I put the panel in with the raised portion up, mark the panel, remove it and then plane, scrape and sand the panel so it's flush with the drawer slips. With the more traditional raised panel, I position the panel bevel-side down.

Keeping the drawer bottom in place—I don't glue drawer bottoms in place. It's

easier to repair a drawer if the bottom just slides right out. To keep solid-wood drawer bottoms from sagging, I screw them to the drawer back with a single pan-head screw and elongate the hole so the bottom can move (see the drawing detail above).

In spite of its strength, a ¼-in. plywood panel is quite flexible, so I usually drive two or three screws into the drawer back. Otherwise, the bottom will sag (see the drawing at right on the facing page).

Another possibility for plywood is to enclose it on all four sides (see the top photo on the facing page). Because plywood is dimensionally stable, there's no need to leave the back open.   □

Gary Rogowski teaches woodworking and is a professional woodworker living in Portland, Ore.

A blend of machine work and handwork produces traditional-style quarter columns. *After turning a blank down to a cylinder and adding a double-bead detail on each end, Mac Campbell reeds the column with a scratch stock while it's mounted on the lathe.*

Quarter Columns Dress Up Boxy Cases
How to make and inset a traditional corner detail

by Mac Campbell

Inset quarter columns add interest to an otherwise plain or boxy carcase. In addition to providing decoration through reeding or other surface detailing, quarter columns, like pilasters on a building, supply a strong visual framework. From the front, a viewer sees an element with some mass, rather than just the edge of a side panel framing a piece's drawers or doors. And since these columns are inset into the corners, instead of the face of a piece, they also relieve the blank expanse of wood commonly found in casework sides.

Best of all, quarter columns aren't difficult to make, and the procedures can easily apply to less traditional column forms for casework corners or even for architectural woodworking. To show how this corner treatment can add a distinctly classical motif to an otherwise ordinary period piece, I'll describe how I prepared and shaped a pair of reeded columns for a traditional-style chest of drawers (see the photo at right). Also, to underline the basic methods involved in insetting quarter columns, I'll explain how I framed and installed them in the chest.

Quarter columns as a whole

The best way that I've found to make quarter columns is to form a full column blank by gluing up four identical pieces of square stock with newspaper between each joint. Then the blank is mounted on the lathe, and its central section is turned to a cylinder with a pair of beads at each end, which define the transition from the cylinder to the square ends. (These beads become the column's base and capital.) If the column is to be reeded or fluted, this work is done before removing the column from the lathe (see the photo on the opposite page). Finally, the column is separated into quarters and two of them are cut to length and installed at the carcase's front corners.

Choosing and gluing up four quarters

Even though there are no strict rules for column size, I've found that 2-in.-dia. columns are the right proportion for a 30-in.- to 36-in.-high piece of furniture, like my hall chest. If you use a 2-in.-dia. column body, you'll need a 2⅜-in.-dia blank to allow for the top and bottom beads and for squaring up the blank after glue-up. To make up a column blank, surface four pieces of your chosen stock. For my chest, I selected mahogany stock that measures 1⁵⁄₁₆-in.-sq. by 4-in. longer than the finished column length. Select stock with a straight grain that's free from unusual grain patterns. Swirls and other striking figures won't show up well because of the column's vertical lines, and they will make hand-reeding much more difficult.

Before gluing up the four pieces to form the column, make sure that each of the four corners to be glued together are exactly 90°. Then spread glue on both pieces of wood, and lay a single layer of newspaper between them before clamping. Since the glued surfaces will have to be scraped clean later, choose a glue that sands well when dry (I use High-Performance PVA from Lee Valley Tools Ltd., 1080 Morrison Dr., Ottawa, Ont., Canada, K2H-8K7). I like to glue up the stock in two pairs, joint one face of each glued-up pair, and then glue those faces together. Once the glue is fully dry (preferably overnight), dress all four sides so that the blank measures 2⅜ in. sq., and the gluelines are still centered.

Although it has never happened to me, it is possible that a turning tool's edge could dig into the spindle (column) and break apart its paper-and-glue joints, sending wood all over the shop. Therefore, as a safety measure and as some cheap insurance against having your work ruined, I recommend screwing the four clamped pieces together. I drive two screws each way near both ends, but well away from the ends of the usable column (see the photo on the facing page).

Reeded quarter columns, inset in corner ledger strips, lend a bold, yet elegant touch to the front of the author's 30-in.-high chest of drawers (above). The carcase relies on period details, like the columns, cock beading, carved feet and brass pulls to offset its otherwise simple box form.

Hand-scraped vertical lines are the effect that the author intended for this chest's corners (right). The beads at the top and bottom serve as the column's capital and base. To clean out the ends of the reeds that the scratch cutter won't reach, Campbell uses a ⅛-in. skew chisel, which further enhances the work's hand quality.

Turning and shaping a full column

Mount the turning blank on the lathe with both the headstock and tailstock centers aligned at the glue-joint intersection. Turn the column round (except for the ends); then turn the top and bottom beads. Although most of the cylinder's surface will be removed during the reeding process, sand the column at this stage to remove small irregularities that might deflect the reeding cutter. To reed the column, you'll need an indexing head for your lathe with at least 24 divisions (48 is preferable). If your lathe doesn't have a built-in indexer, you can rig up one. (See the sidebar on p. 47 on reeding with a scratch stock.)

Quartering a column

After the column is reeded, remove it from the lathe and withdraw the safety screws from the ends of the blank. To divide the column back into quarters, hold the column upright on the floor, and tap a chisel into one of the gluelines (see the photo on p. 46). The seams part quite easily, leaving a layer of paper and glue on each surface, which can be cleaned with a scraper, sander or anything that removes the hardened glue.

Run the growth rings diagonally from the inside corner to the outside corner when laying out the legs. With this orientation, the grain flows with the cabriole curve.

Don't cut the waste completely free of the blank. *Leave a small connecting bridge so waste pieces don't need to be taped or nailed back into place when the stock is rotated to saw the other face.*

tasks. As an independent craftsman, my apprentices are machines that prepare stock quickly so that I can devote my time to the critical hand skills that set this piece apart from factory-made furniture. Fine carving, hand-cut dovetails and handplaned surfaces remove any trace of the machines that did the grunt work before me. Economic reality has taught me that even though I can replicate a period piece of furniture, I can't slavishly follow every method of the Colonial makers.

Building this highboy is well within the abilities of the serious amateur cabinetmaker. (This article deals with the lower case. In the next two issues of *FWW*, we'll build the rest of the highboy—see the box on p. 57.) Although it may appear daunting, much of the work amounts to executing just a few traditional joinery techniques over and over. With so many pieces to cut and assemble (see the drawing on p. 53), organization is as important as technique.

Select stock carefully

All the curly cherry flat stock needs to finish out at ⅞ in. thick, so I usually start with roughsawn, 1⅛-in. stock. The gooseneck molding and lower finials are made from 8/4 curly cherry stock, and I use sound 12/4 straight-grained stock for the legs and the top finials.

All secondary wood is poplar, except drawer bottoms. All internal frame parts are ⅞-in.-thick stock to match the cherry. Drawer sides and backs are ⅝-in.-thick poplar, back

boards are ½ in. thick and drawer bottoms are ⅜-in. aromatic cedar.

Before cutting any wood, select the best figured stock for the most prominent areas: the drawer fronts, the front apron and the wide scroll board at the top of the upper case. Careful stock selection provides a kind of visual rhythm to the piece, uniting upper and lower cases. If I can, I use boards from the same log.

Start by shaping the legs

Even when empty, this is a heavy piece of furniture. Leg strength is important. That's why I look for sound, straight-grained stock to rip into 2¾-in.-sq. leg blanks. Make the blanks an inch longer at the upper end so the lathe drive center has material to bite into. This extra inch of stock will be cut off later, after the leg is shaped and mortised. When laying out the leg profile, align the blanks so the annual rings run diagonally from the inside corner to the outside corner (see the photo above left). This makes the strongest possible leg as well as the most attractive one. The grain lines flow with the contour of the cabriole shape.

First make a full-sized template of the cabriole leg profile on thin plywood or hardboard. Using this template, mark out the leg profile on all four blanks. Before bandsawing the cabriole profile, I define the shoulder line at the junction of the upper post and the curve of the knee. All I do is crosscut the two outside faces of each leg on the tablesaw to a depth just shy of the finished surface.

Only the foot is turned. *With the leg still mounted in the lathe, shape it with a spokeshave and rasp.*

Careful bandsawing makes sculpting the leg much easier. When bandsawing the cabriole profile, I don't saw off the waste completely. Instead, I leave a small, connecting bridge between the leg and the waste. This gives the leg good support as I make the cuts on each face of the leg (see the photo at left). Finally, I return to the first face, and cut through the remaining bridged segments. This bridging method ensures perfect alignment of the sawn faces with the template and eliminates the fussy process of reattaching the sawn waste in some other way to make all the cuts.

Once the leg is sawn to rough shape, mark the centers on both ends of the blank, and turn the foot on the lathe. Be sure to make a crisp top edge on the foot (see the bottom photo on the facing page). This gives a nice reference edge from which to rasp and file the shape.

From this point, I shape the rest of the cabriole profile by hand, using the lathe as a vise to hold the stock. I start with a spokeshave to remove a lot of waste quickly. For shaping, though, a pattern-maker's rasp gives the best results. Finally, I use files and sandpaper to finish the curved leg and foot. Leave edges at the knees sharp, and be careful not to round over any edges where the knee blocks will be attached.

Mortise the leg posts

At this point, the upper part of the leg has been laid out but is still 2¾ in. sq. This is when I lay out and cut the mortises for the back, sides and all three front rails. The full width of the leg stock (see the top photo at right) and the extra inch of length provide stable support for the router. I use a plunge router fitted with a spiral up-cut bit. The bit diameter is slightly smaller than the finished mortise width so that I can shave the cut exactly to my scribed lines. After plunging the mortises, pare to the layout lines, and square up the inside corners with a chisel.

Once all the mortises are cut, rip and crosscut the upper leg posts to size. Stay outside the layout line by about 1⁄16 in. The excess will be planed flush with the sides after assembly. Also, be sure to mark and save the waste pieces from the upper part of the legs. These pieces will be used for making the knee blocks and will give the best possible grain match with the leg.

Prepare the stock for the carcase

Loggers in my area call me when they find an exceptional tree—one that is big, straight and, if I'm lucky, figured. I have to act fast, though, because it's always a race against the veneer-log buyers who also want dazzling wood. Midway through this project, I had to drop everything and dash off to the woods to check out a tip. But that's how I get the figured wood I need for my furniture.

Start by sawing the rough wood so that it's a few inches longer than needed and about ½ in. wider. Normally, I'd surface one face and true up one edge on the jointer and move to the thickness planer. Highly figured wood like this, though, is prone to tearout, so I do the final thicknessing on a wide-belt sander. Later, I'll hand-plane and scrape all the parts to clean up the fuzzy sanded surface and get the silky, hand-worked texture that's so essential to period furniture. Tool marks reveal an intimacy between wood and maker. But to me, it really doesn't matter whether the stock initially was thicknessed by a power planer or with scrub and jack planes.

Cut out the front rails, sides and back

Three tenons connect each case side and the back with the legs, making for some 17 in. of cross-grain construction. With seasonal

A plunge router with a spiral bit roughs out the mortises. The full stock width of the blank provides support for the router.

After the router, use a chisel to pare and square the mortises to the scribed lines.

Cutting tenons by the batch saves time. Clamping the runners and kickers together also makes it easier to keep tenons uniform.

Mark the shoulder line on the narrow edge of each tenon. Cut the waste away on the bandsaw.

Plane the upper leg posts flush with the front. A file, chisel and scraper help to bring all the leg posts flush with the front, sides and back.

Interior rails glued to the front rails and back board reinforce the case and permit longer tenons to be used on drawer runners and kickers.

Dry-fit all parts to find potential problems before glue is applied.

humidity changes, there's a strong possibility of a crack developing in the sides or the back. None of my furniture has developed any cracks, but it is quite common on original pieces. Because a crack along the grain of a side or back doesn't affect structural integrity and gives a look of authenticity, I don't worry about it.

With stock for the sides and back cut to their finished width and length, I use the router and edge guide to start the tenons by cutting a long tongue in each end of the sides and back.

Next lay out and cut the individual tenons with the bandsaw, and then use a chisel to pare the ragged bandsaw cuts to the shoulder lines. Don't cut the bottom scroll yet. Wait until the joints have been dry-fit.

The three horizontal front rails (including the apron) are cut from a single board. Mark the stock to keep the rails in sequence. For these parts, it's easier to lay out and cut the tenons first before ripping the stock into individual rails.

Sides, back and rails should be test-fitted to the legs. If all fits well, take the case apart. Using full-sized patterns, lay out the scroll on the bottom edge of the apron, sides and back. Bandsaw to shape, and clean up the sawn surfaces with a spokeshave and rasp.

The center area on the apron is recessed (or blocked) to align with the fan carving on the drawer above it. Remove the bulk of the waste in this area with the bandsaw, and then finish with a rasp and scraper. Drill the two ½-in.-dia. holes in the bottom of the apron for the turned tenons of the drop finials.

The two vertical dividers between the three lower drawers are milled to size and a dovetail cut on each end. The divider is ⅞ in. deep, but the dovetail only extends ½ in. deep. Fit these pieces to the middle rail and apron after the front legs and rails are glued up.

Make the interior framing members

Along with the parts already made, the case needs additional framing to reinforce joints and support the drawers. The next step is to cut stock for the drawer runners and kickers. Collect all of these pieces, and cut the tenons on the ends at one time (see the third photo from the top on p. 55).

Leg post-to-rail joint strength is my chief concern, so I reinforce this area with interior rails that are notched around the inside corners of the posts. These pieces are glued to both the front rails and the back of the case.

There are three pairs of interior rails. The front interior rails are made of cherry to match the front rails. The back rails are made of poplar. With the exception of the wood species, they are identical. Group the rail pairs. Lay out and cut all the mortises first, and then fit the tenons.

Assemble the base in three stages

A sure way to induce a panic attack is by trying to glue all the parts at once. Having a bunch of glue-slathered parts dripping everywhere is bad enough, but with so many parts to handle, glue can

Glue the rough-shaped knee blocks in place. After the glue dries, use chisels, rasps and sandpaper to blend the entire knee.

Attach the knee blocks

Knee blocks provide a graceful transition between the legs and neighboring surfaces. You'll need six blocks: two each on the three sides that show. Using a template, lay out the profile on leg-post offcuts. Bandsaw the block profile, dress surfaces that butt against the leg and side or apron, and rough shape the curve. Now glue the knee blocks in place (see the photo above). Clamping pressure must squeeze the knee block into the flat on the leg blank and the apron and side. After the glue has dried, fair the entire knee area with carving tools, rasps, files and sandpaper. Some excess wood still must be removed on the inside curve of all four legs so that they'll blend with the apron scroll.

Fit the tenon pins

After sanding the case, drill holes in the leg posts for the tenon pins. They should be made of riven (split) oak. A riven pin is less likely to split or break. Spokeshave the pin with a slight taper to give a tight fit. Before driving them into place, test-fit the pins in a scrap block. Cut these pins slightly proud of the surface using a piece of sandpaper as a gauge, and peen the ends to give an aged look. □

Randall O'Donnell is a period furnituremaker living in the countryside near Bloomington, Ind.

start to set before all the joints are seated and the case squared up. So I begin with just the front assembly. Glue up the two front legs and the three front rails. Be sure to check that the assembly remains square after the clamps are in place (for more on this, see *FWW* #113 pp. 68-71).

After the glue has cured, use a jointer plane, chisel and a rasp to fair the leg posts flush with the rails (see the top left photo on the facing page). Now position the two vertical dividers over the middle rail and apron, and scribe and cut the dovetails. The dividers can now be glued into place.

The backboard is glued up with the back legs, clamped and allowed to dry. Once the back assembly has been removed from the clamps, fair the back leg posts flush with the back.

Once you've glued the interior rails on the front and back assemblies (see the bottom left photo on the facing page), dry-fit the sides and all the drawer runners and kickers. If everything fits well, apply glue to all the mortises and tenons, and bring the whole assembly together and clamp. This operation may take extra hands. Two people certainly make the assembly less nerve-racking.

Be sure that the case remains square after the clamps are tightened. After the glue has dried, clean up any glue squeeze-out, and then fair the leg posts flush with the case sides.

Now install drawer-side guides, which prevent the drawers from cocking when pushed into place. The guides are pieces of poplar, glued and nailed (as was done on the originals) to the runners.

With the lower case complete, the next step is building the graceful upper cabinet that crowns this highboy. Randall O'Donnell details that project in the article on pp. 58-65. The last of the three articles in this series, on pp. 66-72, covers the finials and carved fans.

Curly Cherry Highboy

Making the upper case, drawers and gooseneck molding

by Randall O'Donnell

Earlier in my career, I built kitchen cabinets. At that time, dovetailing meant using a jig and router. I dovetailed more than a thousand drawers that way. But when I decided to become a period furnituremaker, I knew those days were over—only hand-cut dovetails would do. Abandoning the speed of a jig for tedious handwork seemed crazy at first, but with my first hand-cut joint, I learned it wasn't as hard as I thought.

Dovetail joinery is a large part of what goes into constructing the upper case of this highboy. With its bonnet top and graceful moldings, this chest of drawers appears to be a formidable project. But stripped of embellishment, it's simply a large dovetailed box containing smaller dovetailed boxes.

Finding high-quality, wide stock was my biggest challenge. I was fortunate to find outstanding curly cherry. I used poplar for all the secondary wood except the drawer bottoms, where I used aromatic cedar. Using cedar is more work because it involves joining narrow stock, but the wonderful smell that escapes as you open a drawer makes the effort worthwhile.

I described my approach for building the base unit in the article on pp. 52-57. Now I'll detail construction of the upper case (see the photo at left). That involves making the carcase, framing the bonnet top, making the drawers and carving the curved crown, or gooseneck, molding.

Building the basic box

It's virtually impossible to find a single board of figured wood wide enough for the sides. But two well-matched boards glued together look fine. The first step is to glue up stock for the case top, bottom and sides. A piece of furniture like this needs stock that's slightly thicker than what's usu-

An American classic—The dovetailed upper case of this bonnet-top highboy is capped by a sweeping gooseneck molding, which is made with hand and power tools. Construction of the lower case, including its cabriole legs, was covered in the article on pp. 52-57.

ally used on case pieces. I use ⅞-in.-thick stock for the entire case, internal framing and drawer fronts.

I start by flattening one face and jointing one edge of each board. Then I thickness plane the boards to within 1/16 in. of their final thickness. Next, on the tablesaw, I rip the boards to width. I usually don't bother to joint the boards after ripping because I've found that with a good blade and a true-running saw arbor, it's not necessary.

Now I glue up the boards. Once the glue has dried, I sand the pieces to thickness on a wide belt sander. Later, after all the joinery has been cut, I'll surface all the sides, inside and out, with a handplane and cabinet scraper. This gives a handworked texture.

The case is joined at the corners with through dovetails (see the photo at right). The top corners are hidden by the moldings and bonnet, and the bottom corners are covered by the base and the waist molding. This doesn't mean you should be less careful in the joinery, but it does relieve some of the pressure. Flat and square boards make dovetailing easier (for more on dovetailing, see *FWW* #116, pp. 81-86).

After cutting the dovetails on all four corners, I lay the sides on the bench so I can mark the location of the dadoes that will house the drawer runners (see the drawing on p. 60). Using a router, I cut ⅞-in.-wide by ⅛-in.-deep dadoes across the width of the sides.

A rabbet runs around the back inside edge of the case to house the back boards. Using a router, I rabbet the top and bottom pieces across their entire length. The rabbet on each side piece, though, is stopped so that it doesn't break through the outside of the case. Rounded corners can be squared up with a chisel.

The last thing to do on the case is prepare it for the scroll board, the decorated piece at the top of the case. With a router, cut the slots in the top front inside faces of the sides to house the scroll-board tenons. The front edge of the top must be ripped to its finished width to allow the scroll board to slide into place.

Installing runners and rails

With the bulk of the joinery on the case sides completed, it's time to make the inte-

THE BASIC BOX

It's really not complicated. *The upper case of the highboy starts as a large dovetailed box. Molding covers the joinery at top and bottom.*

The top is ⅞ in. narrower than the sides to clear the scroll board at the front of the case.

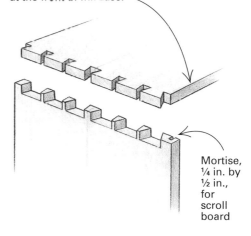

Mortise, ¼ in. by ½ in., for scroll board

Case back is rabbeted for the back boards.

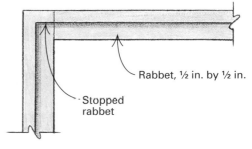

Rabbet, ½ in. by ½ in.

Stopped rabbet

Joinery details

The highboy uses simple dovetail and mortise-and-tenon joinery. This exploded view identifies all the parts used in this part of the highboy.

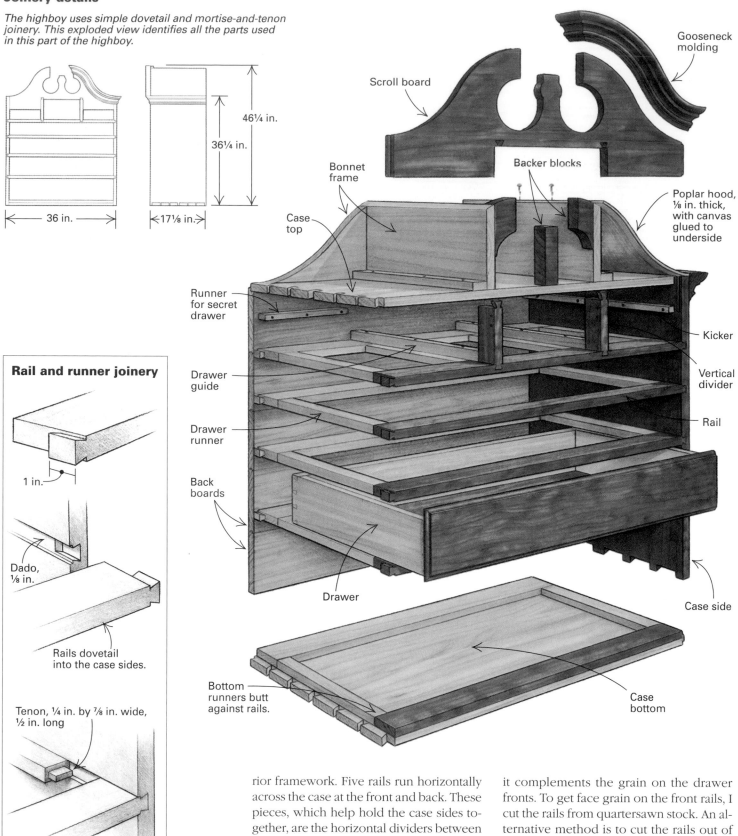

46¼ in.

36¼ in.

36 in.

17⅛ in.

Scroll board

Gooseneck molding

Backer blocks

Bonnet frame

Case top

Poplar hood, ⅛ in. thick, with canvas glued to underside

Runner for secret drawer

Kicker

Drawer guide

Vertical divider

Drawer runner

Rail

Back boards

Drawer

Case side

Bottom runners butt against rails.

Case bottom

Rail and runner joinery

1 in.

Dado, ⅛ in.

Rails dovetail into the case sides.

Tenon, ¼ in. by ⅞ in. wide, ½ in. long

Runners are housed in dadoes in the case sides. The ends of the runners tenon into the rails.

rior framework. Five rails run horizontally across the case at the front and back. These pieces, which help hold the case sides together, are the horizontal dividers between the drawers.

It would be easier to cut the front rails out of ⅞-in.-thick flatsawn cherry, but this would put the edge grain on the front of the chest between the drawers. I prefer the look of face grain on the front rails because

it complements the grain on the drawer fronts. To get face grain on the front rails, I cut the rails from quartersawn stock. An alternative method is to cut the rails out of 12/4 flatsawn stock, but quartersawn stock is more economical.

I start by ripping the rails to 2¾ in. wide and then cutting them to length. I group the rails into front-and-back pairs and lay out the ¼-in.-wide, ⅞-in.-long mortises

Drawings: Bob La Pointe

Slide scroll board into place (above). Make sure that the bottom edge is parallel with the rail below.

Lay out vertical dividers. Scribe the dovetails in the ends of the dividers into the scroll board and rail (right).

Scroll-board pattern

To lay out the scroll board, use the grid pattern to make a full-size template on thin plywood.

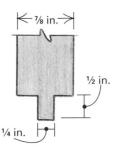

⟵ ⅞ in. ⟶

½ in.

¼ in.

Scroll-board tenon

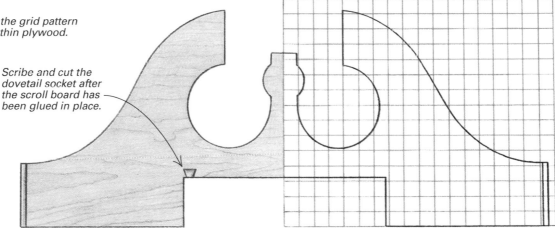

Scribe and cut the dovetail socket after the scroll board has been glued in place.

1 sq. = 1 sq. in.

that will accept the tenons on the ends of the runners. I use a plunge router with a spiral, up-cut bit to cut the mortises ½ in. deep, and then I square up the corners with a chisel.

In the ends of the upper four rail pairs, I make 1-in.-deep dovetails. They'll slide into dovetail sockets that I'll cut after the case is assembled. The bottom rail doesn't need to be held in place by joinery. The rail is simply glued to the case bottom.

The runners, which complete the interior framing, are tenoned into the rails. I group all these parts together and cut the tenons in one setup (for more on this, see the article on pp. 52-57).

Dry-fit the case before gluing

Before applying glue, it's best to dry-fit the case members. Any problems should be corrected now. When the pieces fit correctly, I glue up the box, and then I make sure that the case is square (for more on clamping and squaring cases, see *FWW* #113, pp. 68-71).

After the clamps have been removed, I slide the rails into their respective locations and scribe the dovetails into the case sides. With the case on its back, I chop the dovetail sockets for each front rail. Then I place

Trace the curve of the scroll board onto stock for the rear framing member.

Hold the bonnet frame square, and drill pilot holes for screws. Once the glue has dried, screws are replaced with forged nails.

Scribe the curve on the center wall using the scroll-board template.

the case face down and chop the rear dovetail sockets. I can now glue the front rails in place and allow the glue to set. Next I lay the case face down, glue the drawer runners into the front rails and apply glue to just the front 2 in. of the runner in the dado in the case sides. I don't glue the runners to the back rails, so the case sides can expand and contract freely with humidity changes. Now I glue the back rails in place. And, finally, I glue the bottom drawer rail to the case bottom.

The drawer kickers behind the scroll board prevent the top outside drawers from tipping when they are pulled out. Because these kickers do not carry much weight, they are glued and nailed to the interior case sides with cut nails, as was done on many Early American pieces. Because of the cross-grain construction, I apply glue only along the front half of the kicker.

Scroll board completes the case work

The scroll board is cut from stock that is 14¼ in. wide. Although a single, full-width board is nice, you can join two narrower boards. For the best appearance, though,

Fair the center walls to the scroll curve. Using a handplane, the author works from front to rear to prevent chipping the scroll board.

one of the boards should be at least 11¾ in. wide so that the glue joint is hidden by the gooseneck molding. Before cutting the stock, I make a full-size pattern of the scroll board from thin plywood.

It's easier to cut the tenons on the ends of the scroll board and make the center drawer opening while the board is rectangular. I cut the tenons with a router and a spiral bit and edge guide. Then I bandsaw the rough opening for the center drawer.

I use a router fitted with a flush-trimming bit and a template to make the finish opening, and I clean out the two corners with a chisel. I bandsaw the profile at the top of the scroll board and then smooth it on my belt sander.

With the scroll cut, I lay out and carve the circular fan in the plinth (carving for this highboy will be explained on pp. 66-72). Once the glue is applied to the tenons, the scroll board can be slid into place (see the photo at left on p. 61).

The next step is to fit the vertical dividers for the top center drawer opening. I cut the dividers to size and dovetail the ends first. Although the divider is 2¾ in. deep, the dovetail is only ½ in. deep. I scribe the dovetails to the rail and scroll board (see the photo at right on p. 61), cut the dovetails with a fine backsaw and chisels, and glue the dividers into place.

Riven oak pins anchor the inner edge of the scroll board to the dividers. I drill two ¼-in. holes through each divider and into the edge of the scroll board. I put a little glue on the edge of the pins and drive the pins into the holes, cutting any bit of protruding pin flush with the surface. The upper carcase is now ready for the bonnet framework and thin bonnet top and the gooseneck molding.

Framing the bonnet

The scroll board establishes the curve of the bonnet, but additional framing is needed to enclose this area and support the hood. The first step is to copy the curve from the front scroll board (see the top left photo on the facing page) and to cut the two poplar pieces to shape. Next I cut the stock for the center walls and the cleats that will attach the frame to the case top, and then I glue these pieces together.

I use screws to clamp the parts together temporarily (see the center left photo on the facing page). I replace the screws later with forged nails. The bonnet's frame, like many other traditionally made pieces, does have some cross-grain construction. The

SHAPING THE GOOSENECK MOLDING

Removing waste quickly— *A router does the heavy work quickly. The author will hand-carve the details in this traditional deep molding.*

Custom-made router bits *establish the overall profile of the gooseneck molding.*

Use a gouge that matches the cove radius. *The router-cut blank leaves guide marks for the width and depth of the cove.*

Molding in three steps

Step 1

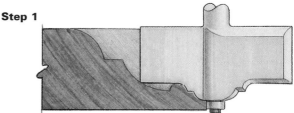

Stock removed by first bit.

Step 2

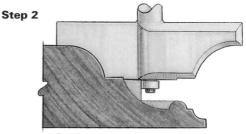

Stock removed by second bit.

Step 3

Shape with gouges.

Clamp the molding in place, and scribe the miter locations (above).

Screws hold the molding to the fence so that the molding can be accurately and safely mitered (right).

Locate the molding ¼ in. above scroll board (above).

Test-bend the hood over the frame. To control cracking, glue canvas to the inside of the hood before it's nailed to the bonnet frame (right).

nails accommodate the wood's seasonal movement without sacrificing strength.

After the glue has dried, I use my hand-plane to fair the center walls with the curve of the scroll board (see the photo at right on p. 62).

Gooseneck molding is routed and then carved

This traditional molding profile has an astragal bead that stands proud of a large cove, creating a dramatic shadow line. I've made a variety of architectural moldings on my shaper, but this profile, with its S-curve shape, is best worked by a combination of router and carving tools.

I start with a full-size pattern to lay out the S-curve on a wide piece of 1½-in.-thick stock. Then I bandsaw and smooth the inside curve to the layout line. I had a pair of router bits made to remove the bulk of the waste quickly (see the center photo on p. 63). The pilot bearing of the first bit follows the inside curve of the blank (see the top photo on p. 63) and creates part of the profile (see the drawing on p. 63). The pilot bearing of the second bit follows the shoulder cut made by the first bit and removes more material.

The remaining material is removed with carving tools, and the entire molding profile is lightly sanded. Finally, I bandsaw the outside curve to separate the molding from the blank and sand the curve to the layout line. The straight moldings for the case sides are made in the same manner.

Mount the molding, and install the hood

The top edge of the molding extends about ¼ in. above the scroll board curve to form a rabbet for the front edge of the hood. To locate the miters, I clamp the molding stock in place and scribe the inner edge of the miter.

Mitering the curved molding can be tricky. To hold it in place securely, I screw the molding to the wooden fence on my miter saw. The straight molding is cut by placing the stock upside down with the back edge against the fence. Once the molding is cut, I drill holes and nail it into place with forged finish nails. The plinth and the upper arch of each scroll have fragile short-grain sections that need reinforcement, so I glue backer blocks behind each of them.

The hood is an 18½-in.-wide poplar board that I plane to ⅛ in. thick. It is bent over the frame and nailed in place (see the photo at left). Most antique hoods have

Make the drawers *after the case work is completed. Batch like parts to speed up the work and produce more consistent results.*

Secret drawers add a little mystery. *The drawers slide toward the center and can be withdrawn from the case.*

cracks in this thin piece of wood, and a few minor splits are unavoidable. But to prevent major cracks, I glue canvas to the underside of the hood with contact cement. This makes a ply construction, and so far, none of my bonnets have any serious cracks. Minor cracks seem to be confined to the ends.

On the home stretch with drawers, backboards

Once the top and bottom cases have been assembled, I make the drawers. After I select the most highly figured boards for the drawer fronts, I make sure that the growth rings on the stock of all the drawers have the same orientation (the faces closest to the bark are all in or all out). Don't mix them up because I've found that the sapwood side will never darken quite as much as the heart, even when the wood comes from the same log.

I cut all the drawer fronts to size, run a bead around the entire drawer front and rabbet the top and sides for a lip—there's no lip on the bottom edge. I check the fit of each drawer and make adjustments. Prior to cutting the dovetails, I carve the fans on the two middle drawer fronts.

Batch all the drawer parts, and lay out and cut the dovetails (for more on drawers, see *FWW* #104, p. 65). The cedar bottoms are fitted after drawers have been glued up. During glue-up, I use a temporary plywood bottom with corners cut off to help square the drawer and to make it easier to clean glue out of the corners.

Even though each drawer front has been fitted to its openings, I work each drawer lightly with a handplane after assembly. A little fussing is usually all that is needed to make each drawer fit perfectly.

Secret compartments add an air of mystery, and this highboy has several. I added two secret drawers inside the case above the two small drawers at the top; they're hidden behind the scroll board. Though not deep, the drawers are plenty big enough

for jewelry or documents (see the photo above right). I also made false bottoms in two other drawers. These have a ½-in. space between two drawer bottoms. The upper bottom is completely housed in a groove. The lower bottom slides in from the back. It's held with a loose-fitting nail that can be pulled out with your fingers.

Five individual boards are used to close the back of the case. The ½-in.-thick boards are handplaned inside and out and have tongue-and-groove edges. I fit the boards horizontally across the case and nail them at the ends. □

Randall O'Donnell is a period furniture-maker who lives in the countryside near Bloomington, Ind.

In the next article, Randall O'Donnell describes the carved fans and flame finials that complete this highboy. The article on pp. 52-57 detailed the lower case.

Curly Cherry Highboy

*Flame finials
and carved fans
complete this classic*

by Randall O'Donnell

I magine moving your household and three days later, packing up and moving again. That's what it's like to be an exhibitor at a furniture show. Setting up a booth is hard work. After the carpet was down and everything in place at a recent show, I caught my breath and watched as prospective customers walked into my booth to take a closer look at this highboy. It's almost 7½ ft. tall, and the figure of the curly cherry is exceptional.

Invariably, admirers would walk up to

Photos except where noted: Dennis Preston

UPPER AND LOWER DRAWER FANS

There are three carved fans on this highboy; one on the center drawer of the upper case, one on the center drawer of the base and a third, much smaller, one at the top of the scroll board (see the drawing on p. 71).

Upper fan

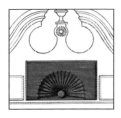

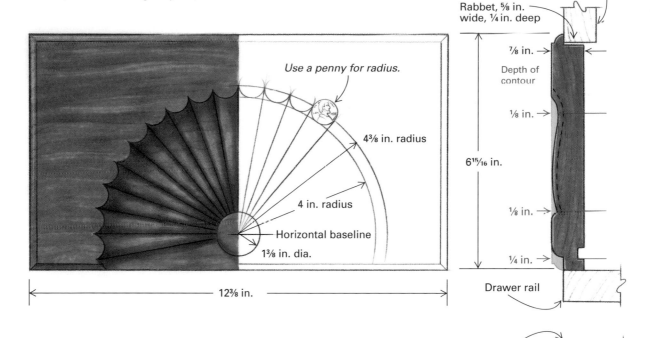

Use a penny for radius.

4³⁄₈ in. radius

4 in. radius

Horizontal baseline

1³⁄₈ in. dia.

12³⁄₈ in.

Scroll board

Rabbet, ⁵⁄₈ in. wide, ¼ in. deep

⁷⁄₈ in.

Depth of contour

⅛ in.

6¹⁵⁄₁₆ in.

⅛ in.

¼ in.

Drawer rail

Lower fan

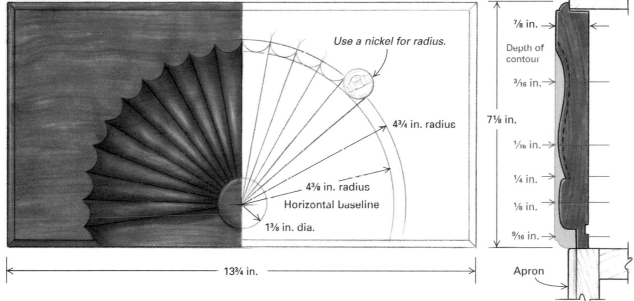

Use a nickel for radius.

4¾ in. radius

4³⁄₈ in. radius

Horizontal baseline

1³⁄₈ in. dia.

13¾ in.

Drawer rail

⁷⁄₈ in.

Depth of contour

³⁄₁₆ in.

7⅛ in.

¹⁄₁₆ in.

¼ in.

⅛ in.

⁹⁄₁₆ in.

Apron

the highboy and somewhat tentatively run their fingers over the fans carved into the two center drawers. Carving seems to serve as the touchstone of a piece (see the photo at left on the facing page). If the carvings look and feel right, customers stay to ask questions, take a brochure and, perhaps, place an order.

I make 18th-century-style furniture. Working within this form, I like to play with the details—to put my stamp on a piece. And nowhere is the ground more

fertile for expressing individuality than in carving. Although I have no reservations about using machines for preparing stock, carving is one of several things that I do completely by hand.

In the two articles on pp. 52-65, I described building the base and upper case of the highboy. Now it's time to carve the fans in the two center drawers and turn and carve the flame finials that crown the bonnet.

This highboy also has two smaller drop

finials in the base and a small, round fan carved in the center of the pediment. These parts use the same carving and turning techniques and are shown in the drawings on p. 71.

Lay out the fans with a compass and coins

The fans (or shells) in the center of the upper chest and lower base are one of the most eye-catching details on a highboy. There are many regional variations. I adapt-

CARVING THE FANS

Fans carved into drawer fronts at the top and bottom of the case help give the highboy its distinctive look. The 20 rays in each fan are laid out and carved on a serpentine background.

1 *A coin for the scalloped edge—A penny is the right size for the upper drawer fan. A nickel fits the lower fan.*

2 *A scribe line marks the depth of the carved surface below the fan. This area forms the transition between the fan and the case rail.*

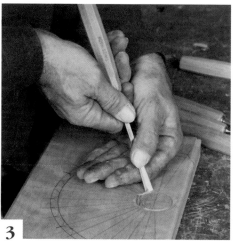

3 *To prevent wood from splintering into the hub surface, outline this area with carving tools.*

4 *Shape the fan background across the grain. Developing the S-shaped surface with mostly cross-grain cutting gives greater control over the tool.*

5 *Smooth the surface with a sculptor's rasp. A uniform surface makes carving the fan's rays easier.*

ed these fans from several Boston pieces.

To lay out a fan, I start by drawing a vertical centerline on the drawer front and then marking the horizontal baseline by eye (see the drawing on p. 67). The intersection of these two lines forms the center point of the fan. From this point, I scribe the outer radius, inner radius and hub diameter with a compass. These lines establish the overall size of the fan.

The fans are sized in proportion to drawer height, and each of these drawer fans has 20 rays. I found that the edge of a coin works well for laying out the ray spacing and scalloped edge. Starting at the center, I lay the coin on one side of the vertical cen-

terline so that the coin just touches the inner radius (see the top left photo above). I trace a semicircle around the coin, stopping at the outer radius.

I continue scribing the semicircles along the length of the arc and then repeat the procedure on the other half of the fan. I use a penny for the upper drawer fan and a nickel for the lower fan. With the spacing established, I draw lines from the center point to the scallops, marking the rays.

Because the lipped drawers stand proud of the case, the fan carving needs a transition to the horizontal rail below the drawer. To do that, I lower the surface of the drawer front immediately below the fan. I

complete the layout by setting the drawer front in the case and scribing a line on the lower edge of the drawer using the rail as a guide (see the top right photo above).

Carve the background and then the rays

A crisp scalloped edge heightens the contrast between the fan and drawer surface. To prevent wood splintering beyond the area being worked, I cut the outline of the hub and scallops into the drawer face with carving tools (see the bottom left photo above). Using a gouge with a sweep that closely matches the curve makes this easy.

The area on which the rays are carved is

From *Fine Woodworking* (July 1996) 119:52-58

6 *Use a bench chisel to remove the waste below the fan.* This surface provides the transition from the carved drawer to the case rail.

7 *A V-parting tool is used to define the rays. Because the surface is S-shaped, wood grain can change direction. Take care not to run tools against the grain, which could cause tearout.*

8 *A successful fan carving is symmetrical. Shape the rays so they appear uniform in width and depth.*

9 *Sand the fan. The scallops and hub should not be rounded over.*

worked with gouges to form a shallow S-profile. This S-contour makes the finished fan sensuous. The serpentine effect can be further accentuated by the depth of the individual rays, so don't hog out too much material at this stage. I get the best results by removing the waste in a series of cuts along the curve. This is mostly cross-grain and skew-cutting (see the bottom center photo on the facing page), which minimizes the chance of taking too much material at once.

Once the bulk of the waste is removed, I smooth the surface with a sculptor's rasp (see the bottom right photo on the facing page). I don't use sandpaper until all carving is completed because grit particles left behind can quickly dull carving tools. Working the surface to the serpentine shape removes most of the ray lines between the hub and the inner radius. Now I redraw them.

The rough-shaping for the ray surface is complete. I now hog out waste below the hub and bottom rays, making the transition to the rail on the carcase. A ⅜-in. bench chisel works well for bringing this surface down to the line scribed earlier in the layout (see the photo at left above).

With the scallops and hub incised and the ray surface formed, I start carving the individual rays. A ray, in cross section, has a

CARVING THE FLAME FINIALS

1

A strip of paper wrapped around the finial creates a helix. The ends of the helices are brought to a point by eye.

2

Begin carving with a narrow veiner. Be careful not to cut into layout lines.

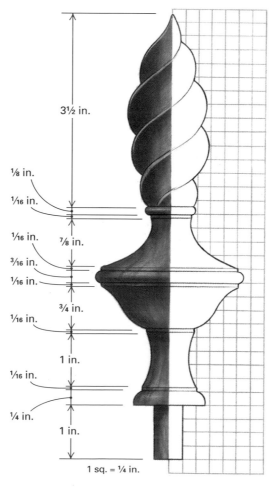

3

To form the flute, remove waste from between the helical grooves with a larger gouge.

Finial layout

Three flame finials cap the top of the upper case. Each has four flutes, which make one complete turn around the finial.

3½ in.

⅛ in.

1/16 in.

1/16 in.   ⅞ in.

3/16 in.

1/16 in.

¾ in.

1/16 in.

1 in.

1/16 in.

¼ in.

1 in.

1 sq. = ¼ in.

crowned shape. The height of the crown remains constant as the ray broadens, expanding from the hub to the scalloped edge. I begin carving the rays by defining the lines with a V-parting tool (see the top right photo on p. 69). Because of the serpentine surface, I have to change the tool direction so that I am always cutting downhill in relation to the grain. This helps me avoid lifting a big chip or having the wood split far ahead of the tool.

I use gouges to shape the rays. Starting from the V on either side, I cut along the ray, gradually working it to a rough convex shape (see the center right photo on p. 69). The faceted surface is smoothed into a continuous curve.

The hub is slightly tapered and crowned, but this detail is carved last. The hub can get nicked if you get too close with a V-parting tool or a gouge. These nicks are cut away with the final shaping. Periodically, I check the rays to make them the same, deepening the V between rays where it's needed. I crown the surface of the hub and taper the sides slightly. Finally, rifflers and sandpaper complete the fan (see the bottom right photo on p. 69).

Flame finials start on the lathe

These finials use the burning-torch motif that's seen on many high chests and tall clocks. The lower part of the finial is an urn, and the twist above it represents a flame. The overall shape is developed on the lathe, and the flame is then carved at the bench. The finials are made of 2¾-in.-sq. cherry stock.

I start by cutting the billets about 2 in. longer than the overall length of the completed finial (see the drawing at left) and then locating the center points for mounting them on the lathe. I turn the finial to shape and use a parting tool to establish the key diameters and gouges to cut and blend the sections together.

I turn a ½-in.-dia. by 1-in.-long tenon on the end of the urn, nearest the headstock. Then I turn the tip of the flame to ¼ in. dia. and sand the entire finial. Even though the flame surface will be carved, a smooth surface makes it easier to lay out the twist.

The flame detail is somewhat like a screw thread—four grooves spiral up from the urn to converge at the tip to a point. Each groove (or flute) makes one complete turn. To lay out the flame, I mark the middle of the length of the turning. Then, using the indexing head on my lathe to hold the stock in position, I make four longitudinal lines at 90° intervals. Using these lines on the flame section, I create the helical flutes by wrapping a strip of paper around the flame portion and scribing a line along the edge of the paper (see the top photo on the facing page). After all four helical lines are drawn, I blend the starting and ending points by eye. Now I can remove the turning from the lathe and saw off the waste at the ends.

Carve the flame with gouges

Holding turned pieces for carving can be a problem. The best solution I've found is to drill a hole slightly smaller than the finial tenon in a piece of scrap the size of a short 2x4 and jam the finial's round tenon into it. I can now clamp the scrap stock in my vise to position the finial at a comfortable angle and height.

I start defining the helix with a narrow gouge (see the center photo on the facing page), and then I work up to a gouge that is slightly smaller than the flute width (see the bottom photo on the facing page). Be careful not to cut into the helical layout line because this will alter the profile of the flame. I work each flute one at a time to avoid any mix-ups. After the flutes are carved, I smooth them with a round rasp and sandpaper.

Make the waist molding

When the fans and finials are completed, it's time to return to the highboy and finish the remaining details: the waist molding, plinths and finial caps.

The waist molding visually eases the transition between the base and the upper case. The molding, on the front and both sides of the case, also has a practical purpose. It keys the upper case to the base. I make the bead-and-cove profile on a shaper (see the waist-molding drawing detail at right). About 7 ft. of stock is needed to frame the front and sides.

To install the molding, I center the upper case on the base with the backs flush. This leaves a 1-in. gap on the front and sides to cover with the waist molding. I now measure and cut the molding stock. The molding is glued and nailed (with 4d cut nails) to the base unit. When the molding is in place, it's not necessary to fasten the upper case to the base.

Make the plinths, and mount the finials

The finials on the upper corners of the bonnet sit atop small pedestals, also called

FINISHING TOUCHES

Scroll-board fan

A carved fan punctuates the top of the scroll board. The fan has an outside radius of 2⅛ in. and a total of 17 rays.

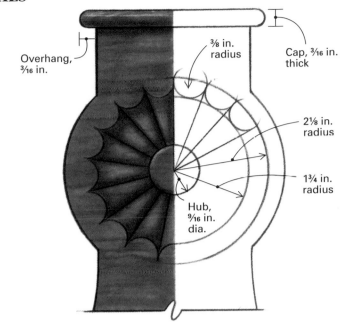

Overhang, ³⁄₁₆ in.

³⁄₈ in. radius

Cap, ³⁄₁₆ in. thick

2⅛ in. radius

1¾ in. radius

Hub, ⁹⁄₁₆ in. dia.

Plinth and finial cap

The plinth and the finial cap provide a base for the finial.

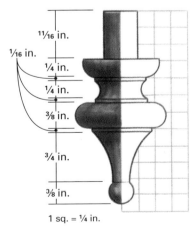

Hole, ½ in., for finial tenon

Full radius

Finial cap, 2 in. sq., ³⁄₁₆ in. thick

Flutes, ⅛ in. by ¹⁄₁₆ in. deep

1 in.

Contour and glue to curved hood.

Plinth, 1½ in. sq.

Waist molding

This molding holds the upper case in place on the base unit. It also provides the visual transition between these two large masses.

1 sq. = ¼ in.

Drop finial

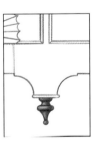

Tenons, ½ in. dia., attach two drop finials to the apron of the highboy's base. The finials are set on cap pieces ³⁄₁₆ in. thick.

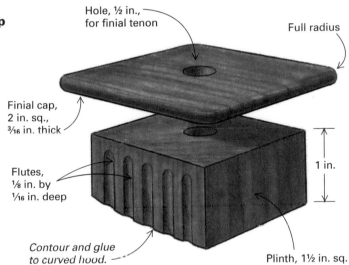

1¹⁄₁₆ in.
¹⁄₁₆ in.
¼ in.
¼ in.
³⁄₈ in.
¾ in.
³⁄₈ in.

1 sq. = ¼ in.

plinths. Each plinth is a 1½-in.-sq. by 1-in.-tall cherry block with a ½-in.-dia. hole bored through the top center for the finial tenon. Five ⅛-in.-wide, evenly spaced flutes are carved into the front face (see the plinth and finial cap drawing on p. 71).

The only trick to making the plinths is scribing the bottom of the plinth block to the curved hood, making certain that the plinth sits plumb. Here's what I do: Because the plinth is rather stubby, I temporarily fit a 2-ft.-long dowel into the hole in the plinth block. I use this long dowel as a sighting device.

I position the plinth block in the corner of the bonnet and, holding the dowel plumb, scribe the block to the bonnet curve. Because there's not much stock to remove to the scribe line, I use my belt sander. Then I glue the plinth blocks to the bonnet hood with contact cement—yellow glue doesn't work as well for this end-grain joint.

All five finials (three upper and two drop finials on the base) sit directly on a plinth cap. Each cap is a small piece of cherry stock, 3/16 in. thick with a full radius on all edges. The caps overhang the bases on which they are mounted by 3/16 in. on each side. A ½-in. hole is bored in the center for the finial tenon, and the caps are glued and nailed with brads to the plinths.

I don't glue the finials in place, so they can be removed when the highboy is moved. They are less likely to break or be damaged that way. Placing the finials on the highboy completes the woodworking portion of this project (see the photo at right on p. 66).

Apply the finish

Finish is such a personal preference. Advocates speak passionately for their favorite finishing materials and techniques. For me, the choice is simple—I use shellac. It's hard to beat for depth, luster and authenticity. Before applying the finish, I wet the surfaces to raise the grain. After the surfaces dry, I sand away the fuzz. I then apply a water-based aniline dye.

If you're unfamiliar with aniline dyes, experiment on scrap first to check the color. These dyes produce beautifully clear and vibrant colors, but they won't behave exactly like the oil-based pigmented stains you may be used to. It's easy to get lap marks if you're not careful. Using several coats of diluted dye is more predictable than trying to get the right color in a single coat.

After the dye is dry, I lightly rub the surface with a Scotch-Brite pad to remove any

THE UPPER CASE

This highboy's dovetailed upper case, with curved gooseneck molding and contoured bonnet, was covered in the article on pp. 58-65.

THE LOWER CASE

Construction of the highboy's lower case, including its cabriole legs, interior framework and carved knee blocks, was described in the article on pp. 52-57.

additional raised grain. I then apply an oil-based glazing stain. Unlike the dye, glazing stain is very forgiving. It evens the base color and gives the look of 100 years of patina. I leave some residue in cracks and crevices to add to the aging effect.

After a 24-hour drying period, I start padding on shellac with a soft cloth. Between each coat of shellac, I lightly sand with a fine Scotch-Brite pad and wipe the surface with a clean cloth. I used four coats of shellac on this highboy. Customers often request a final waxed surface. It certainly imparts a satiny depth, but wax attracts dust and fingerprints and always needs periodic re-waxing. I usually skip it. ☐

Randall O'Donnell is a period furniture-maker who lives in the countryside near Bloomington, Ind.

Visible Joinery Makes a Chest

Flared mortises and jig-cut wedges create matching, tight-fitting through-tenons

by Malcolm Vaughan

Early in the design of a small chest of drawers, I decided to lean in the direction of Arts and Crafts. I wanted the four-drawer bureau to have clean lines and simple edge profiles (see the photo below). As a decorative feature, I decided to wedge the through-tenons on the ends of the drawer dividers with pear, which would contrast with the black walnut I chose for the chest's carcase. I also selected pear for the drawer sides and backs, so the contrast would likewise accentuate the drawers dovetail joinery (see the top photo on the following page). Finally, I picked aromatic cedar for the drawer bottoms and the chest's back panel, which floats in a conventional frame.

Quite a few furnituremakers feel it's extravagant to use solid wood as drawer dividers. But in my chest, I wanted solid dividers, though I didn't cut them from prime timber. In the time it would take me to join and glue-up web frames, I was able to make solid dividers that not only serve as drawer runners but also act as dust boards. And solid dividers allowed me to accent the chest's joinery; I penetrated the two sides with pairs of through tenons at the corners of each of the three dividers and the bottom. This meant I had to make and insert 64 wedges. To speed the job along and help ensure that each of the joints would look alike (see the top photo on p. 74), I came up with a jig to quickly bandsaw indentical wedges. Before I tell you about the wedges, though, I'll describe how I built the rest of the bureau, including how I laid out and routed out each of its 32 slightly flared mortises.

Chest construction

To start any furniture project, I make a dimensioned sketch, a materials list and an order of operations, which usually saves me from cutting pieces the wrong size, gluing parts together too soon and wasting time. For the chest (see the drawing on p. 75), I cut, shaped and fit components and joinery in the following order:

Subtle geometry in this chest of drawers built by Malcolm Vaughan accentuates both the wood and the form, reflecting the honesty in materials and manufacture that is the hallmark of the Arts-and-Crafts style. Vaughan boldly pierced the bureau's side with the through-tenon ends of the drawer dividers, contrasting black walnut tenons with pear wedges.

Sides—Before I edge-jointed the boards for the sides, I tapered the stock's thickness using a carrier jig in my surface planer (I describe a similar jig in *FWW* #95, p. 55). Next I cut the sides to dimension and cleaned up all the surfaces. Then I cut dadoes to support the ends of the dividers, and I rabbeted the edge of the sides to retain the back. To mark out the dadoes, I lightly knifed their positions across both faces of the sides. This makes for accurate mortising later and eliminates tearout around the mortise edges.

Dividers—When I was cutting out the dividers and bottom, I double checked the ends for squareness across their width (if they're not square, subsequent fitting of the drawers is a nightmare). It's actually not a bad idea for a carcase to widen slightly toward the back, and many cabinetmakers build such an "inaccuracy" into their cases.

Bandsawing the tenons—After planing the dividers for a tight fit in the dadoes, I marked off each end for a double pair of tenons. Next I bandsawed the tenon cheeks using a sharp, fine-tooth blade. I guided the edge of each board along the rip fence, and I clamped a stop block to the table to keep from cutting too far. To remove the waste and establish the land between the tenons, I guided my router (fitted with a ¼-in. straight bit and a long fence) along the ends of each board. After routing, I cleaned up the corners with a chisel. Next I hand-sawed the dividers' front shoulders. Finally I went back to the bandsaw to cut slots in the tenons for the wedges, each time setting the rip fence to guide the cut.

Cutting the mortises—To mark out all the mortises, I slid the end of each divider into its corresponding dado, carefully aligning the rear edge with the edge of the rabbet, and then I scribed the locations in the dado using an awl. To mark the mortise locations on the outside face of the side, I again laid the divider in position against the side (close to one of my earlier-made lower dado lines) and nicked positions with my knife.

The real trick to get the wedges to fit uniformly is to flare both sides of each mortise the same amount (¹⁄₁₆ in.) toward the side's outer face (see the drawing detail on the facing page). To mark the flare, I first clamped a straightedge across the outside, close to the lower dado line. Then I took a short piece of stock the same thickness as what would be the flared tenon width, and laid it square to the straightedge. Centering this piece over each tenon location let me knife exactly to where the tenon would spread once it was wedged. Taking a few minutes to accurately mark out at this stage guaranteed that all the wedges would drive into the tenons at the same depth and thus appear uniform in width. I wasted most of each mortise with a router fitted with a ¹⁄₄-in. bit. While I was at it, I routed a mortise in each divider to house drawer stops (see the drawing on the facing page). Finally I chiseled squarely to the lines.

Dry-fitting and shaping—Next came the dry-fitting. I always enjoy this part because it lets me see, for the first time, the piece of furniture taking shape from what started out as a pile of rough-sawn boards. To hold the components in place as I checked the joints for proper fit, I made four sets of side cauls, which I bar-clamped across the width of the case near each row of mortises. The cauls, which have a slightly convex face, ensure that the dividers go fully into their dadoes; without the cauls, the center of the sides might bow outward.

After dismantling the chest, I slightly rounded the front edges of the sides with a plane, checking the profile against a cardboard template. Using an old *Fine Woodworking* "Quick tip," I smoothed the curves with a piece of sandpaper, which was wrapped around a half deck of playing cards. To create shallow feet at the corners, I used my spokeshave to shape and chamfer the bottom of the sides. Then masking off all the joints with tape, I finish-sanded and waxed the chest's inside faces, which would be much more difficult to do after glue-up.

Mass-producing wedges

To cut out the wedges, I returned to my trusty bandsaw to use a shopmade wedge-making jig. The bottom photo above shows how I inserted the corner of my ³⁄₄-in.-thick pear stock (with the grain running across its width) in a corner of the jig's medium-density fiberboard base. After slicing off each wedge, I flipped the wood over and repeated the cut until I piled up enough wedges for the job. Then I regathered my cauls and clamps, and I took a deep breath in preparation for gluing up the dividers into the sides.

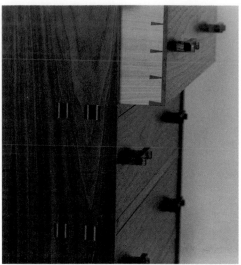

Tight through-tenons—*The author gets uniform and snugly fitting through-tenons by driving the wedges into the tenon slots an equal amount. This requires all the wedges be identical and all the mortises be the same size. It also means the side walls of the mortises must be flared uniformly to correspond to the wedge angle.*

Wedge-o-matic—*Vaughan made a simple jig to bandsaw consistent wedges for 32 through-tenons. To use the jig, he first inserts a corner of a piece of pear (with its grain running across the width) into a notch in the jig's base. Then he slides the base along the fence to slice off a wedge.*

Assembling the case

Initially, I was concerned that knocking in 64 wedges before the glue set up would be a desperate race against the clock. As it turned out, it didn't take long at all. If you're still worried about time, I suggest you use a two-part glue, and dip the wedges in the catalyst part just before you insert them.

Most woodworking textbooks rightly say that wedges should run across the grain and not with it. They also say to drill holes at the end of the tenon slots. Well, I didn't do either of those things on my chest, but I had no problems when installing the wedges. I figured the joints wouldn't split the sides as long as I tapped the wedges into their slots until the tenon just filled the mortise. Of course, you don't want to drive the wedges with a 2-lb. club. I used a light hammer with a face just big enough to simultaneously strike both wedges into a tenon. I stopped tapping when I heard the pitch change as the wedges bottomed out solidly. When all the wedges were home, I cut off their protruding ends and then belt-sanded them flush with the sides.

With the case together, I measured for the chest's top, allowing it to overhang on three sides. When I cut out the top, I sawed the back edge square, but I sloped the overhanging sides by tilting my tablesaw blade to 70°. I hand-shaped the subtle edge curve on these three sides. After rabbeting the top for the back panel, I sanded both the top and the exterior of the sides. Next I drilled holes in the top and sides, and then I doweled and glued the top on.

Pulls, drawers, a back and a finish

It seems whenever two or more furniture-makers get together, the conversation always turns to handles and the restless hours a maker spends trying to integrate pulls into an overall design. I, too, have a healthy stash of failed handle mock-ups to kindle a fire during the winter. But I was pleased with the pulls I came up with for this chest of drawers (see the drawing detail). The crossbar reflects the shape of the top of the chest, and the ends of the support pieces curve gently, like the front edges of the bureau's sides. One thing to remember: It's much easier to cut mortises or bore holes for the pulls before you glue up the drawers (the four drawers in my chest are dovetailed together the conventional way). This is also a good time to fit the drawer stops (I used ebony) in each divider.

After fitting the drawers, I screwed the chest's frame-and-panel back in place. Once I had the chest completely together, I applied four coats of Danish oil to the outside; the first coat diluted 50% with white spirits for better penetration, the second one straight from the can and the last two applied with a fine-grit (gray) Scotchbrite nylon pad. □

Malcolm Vaughan is a furnituremaker living in Devon, England.

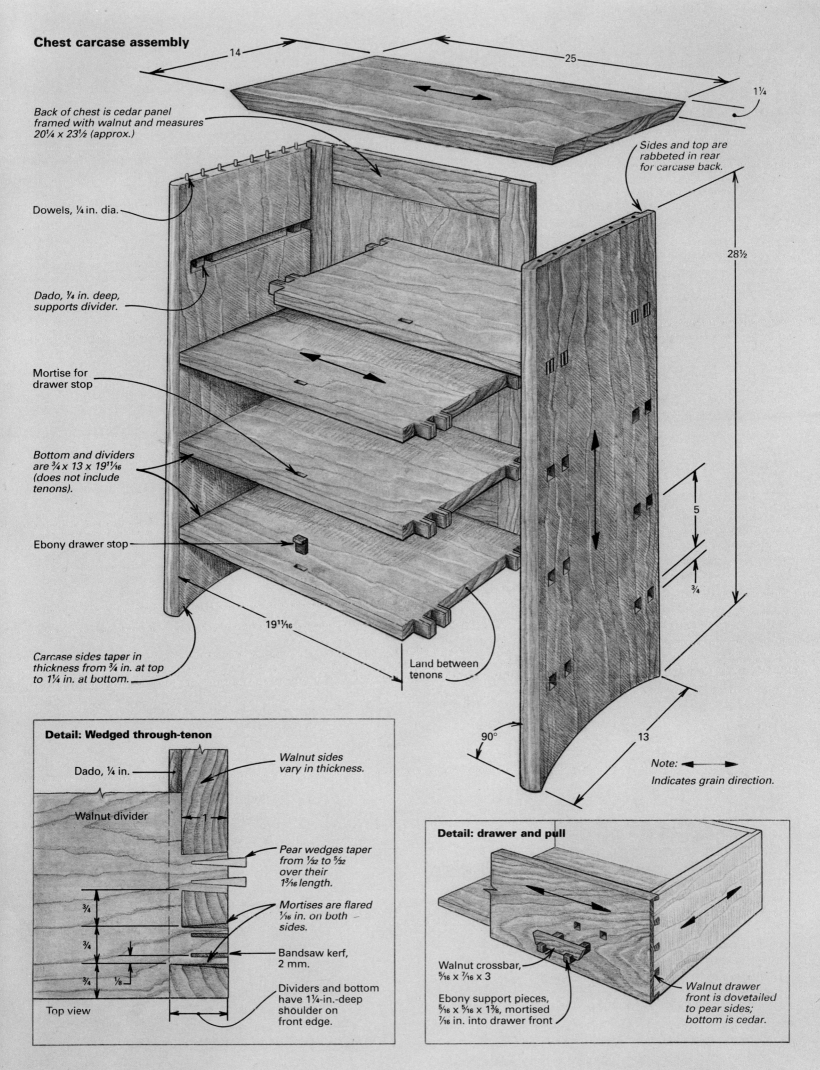

Chest carcase assembly

14

25

1¼

Back of chest is cedar panel framed with walnut and measures 20¼ x 23½ (approx.)

Sides and top are rabbeted in rear for carcase back.

Dowels, ¼ in. dia.

28½

Dado, ¼ in. deep, supports divider.

Mortise for drawer stop

Bottom and dividers are ¾ x 13 x 19¹¹⁄₁₆ (does not include tenons).

5

¾

Ebony drawer stop

19¹¹⁄₁₆

Land between tenons

Carcase sides taper in thickness from ¾ in. at top to 1¼ in. at bottom.

90°

13

Note: Indicates grain direction.

Detail: Wedged through-tenon

Dado, ¼ in.

Walnut sides vary in thickness.

Walnut divider

1

Pear wedges taper from ¹⁄₃₂ to ⁵⁄₃₂ over their 1³⁄₁₆ length.

¾

¾

Mortises are flared ¹⁄₁₆ in. on both sides.

Bandsaw kerf, 2 mm.

¾   ⅛

Dividers and bottom have 1¼-in.-deep shoulder on front edge.

Top view

Detail: drawer and pull

Walnut crossbar, ⁵⁄₁₆ x ⁷⁄₁₆ x 3

Ebony support pieces, ⁵⁄₁₆ x ⁵⁄₁₆ x 1⅜, mortised ⁷⁄₁₆ in. into drawer front

Walnut drawer front is dovetailed to pear sides; bottom is cedar.

Blanket Chest Provides Simple, Stylish Storage

Large finger joints make quick, solid construction

by Gary Rogowski

I have a sweater that's almost as old as I am. I've worn it through sun and storm, through good times and bad. Its wool now holds more memories than warmth, but I can't throw it away. Where to store it and the other sweaters and blankets I have accumulated over the years had started to become a problem. I felt like the world was shrinking, and I needed more storage space.

A blanket chest seemed like the best solution. I kept the design simple so that the piece would be adaptable. I wanted a piece of furniture that would look equally at home in many rooms and with many other styles of furniture.

The construction is simple as well. It's a plank chest with screwed and plugged finger joints. The top is a large panel with breadboard ends, butt hinged to the chest. I wanted a plain, open-grained wood to complement the design, so I decided to use elm. The wood is fairly rare these days because Dutch elm disease has eliminated so many trees, but I found enough nice boards for this chest. For the bottom panel, I chose aromatic cedar, confident it would keep the moths from finishing off my old sweater.

Stock and preliminary surface preparation

I rough milled the stock to within 1/16 in. of its final thickness and matched boards for color and grain. I edge-jointed the boards and dry-clamped them to make sure my joints closed up tight. Because I was using four or five boards per panel, biscuits helped keep my boards aligned during glue-up. After the glue had set up a bit and the squeeze-out had gotten rubbery, I scraped it off.

Photos except where noted: Vincent Laurence

Finger-jointed blanket chest

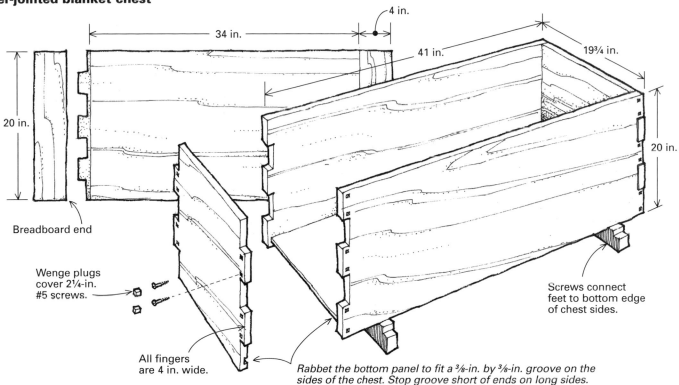

34 in.

4 in.

41 in.

19¾ in.

20 in.

20 in.

Breadboard end

Wenge plugs cover 2¼-in. #5 screws.

All fingers are 4 in. wide.

Screws connect feet to bottom edge of chest sides.

Rabbet the bottom panel to fit a ⅜-in. by ⅜-in. groove on the sides of the chest. Stop groove short of ends on long sides.

Handsome storage, great joinery practice. These large finger joints look great and help make the blanket chest a manageable, not-too-fussy project. Wenge plugs, feet and handle contrast well with the elm.

The panels still needed to be flattened. So I planed and scraped one side of each flat and took the panels to a local shop where I could run them through a wide-belt sander. Then I cut all my pieces to width and length. I was surprised at how much the elm fuzzed when cut, especially when crosscut. To minimize tearout on the final crosscuts, I applied masking tape where the cuts would be.

With the boards at finished size, I scraped the surfaces of all the panels to a nice luster. Then, with a sanding block cut from a small piece of blue-foam building insulation, I lightly hand-sanded the boards with 180-grit sandpaper. I sanded before cutting the joints, so I wouldn't risk rounding over any surfaces near a joint. That finger could result in a sloppy fit.

Joining the carcase

Large finger joints look solid, and they make the piece relatively straightforward to build. There are just four steps to this process: rough bandsawing, template routing, squaring up corners and fitting joints (see the photos on p. 78).

Template simplifies joinery—I started by making patterns from ¼-in. medium-density fiberboard (MDF), which I used to lay out the panels. Later, I used these same patterns as templates for routing. I cut the MDF pieces to the width of the chest's sides. Then I marked out even divisions, so I had three fingers on one template and two on the other, each 4 in. wide. Once the templates fit each other snugly, I laid them on my panels and pencil-marked the joints. I also marked each of the panels for face side and, to prevent confusion, numbered each corner.

Drilling for screws and plugs—Glued finger joints are plenty strong, but a little insurance doesn't hurt. I decided to screw the fingers together and then plug the screw holes. After squaring up the corners of the finger joints, but before fitting them, I drilled two ¼-in. holes in each finger for plugs. I pared the holes square and drilled holes all the way through for the screws.

Once all the finger joints were fitted and the carcase dry-clamped, I started the screws into the finger joints to mark the end grain for drilling. Then I disassembled the carcase and drilled into

CHEST SIDES ARE TEMPLATE ROUTED

Lay out the finger joints with a template. This eliminates the potential for measurement errors and speeds layout.

Photo: Phil Harris

Bandsaw takes out most of the waste. The author removes all but the last 1/16 in. of waste between the fingers.

Template routing ensures consistent results. With a bearing-guided bit and a template, the author produces joints of consistent width and depth. After completing a pass at half-depth, he makes a second pass with the bearing resting on the routed portion of the finger joint.

Photo: Phil Harris

Fitting the joints. The templates are sized so that chest sides will barely go together. This allows for some final fitting.

the end grain with a 7/64-in. bit—about the right diameter for the shank of the 2 1/4-in.-long #5 screws I was using.

Grooving the sides, rabbeting the bottom—I routed a groove near the bottom of the chest for the bottom panel. The groove runs all the way across on the ends but is stopped on the sides. I also routed a rabbet around the bottom panel, so it would fit in the grooves. Then I finished the insides of the four side panels with a couple of coats of shellac, taking care not to let it drip into the joints. I left the bottom unfinished to let the cedar breathe.

Glue-up—With all these surfaces, the glue-up was tricky, so I wanted to simplify things as much as possible. I attached clamping blocks over each finger with double-faced tape and applied a light coat of glue to the end-grain surfaces to seal the pores. I pulled out all the clamps I would need, set them in a convenient place and opened their jaws. Then I quickly swabbed glue onto all the edge-grain surfaces of the finger joints, joined a side and two ends, slid in the bottom panel, attached the other side and clamped up. I checked the inside diagonals of the chest right away to make sure it was square. I cleaned up the glue squeeze-out with a chisel once it had become a little rubbery.

Screwing and plugging the fingers—After the glue had set up, I drove the screws into the fingers. The wenge plugs were cut just a 1/64 in. or so larger than the 1/4-in. plug holes. To make the plugs, I rough-milled the stock on the bandsaw and then, using a push stick and fingerboard, carefully cut it square on the tablesaw. I crosscut the plugs to length—about 3/8 in. long—and handplaned them to size using a bench hook. Then I used a stationary belt sander to put a slight taper on just the bottom third of the plugs. This made it easier to drive them home (see the top photo at right). I chamfered the tops of the plugs with a chisel, paring toward the center (see the photo at right).

Making the top

Breadboard ends are essential to keep a panel the size of this top flat. I decided that the best solution would be to use three discrete tenons with a stub tongue across the entire width of the top (for more on breadboard ends, see *FWW* #110, pp. 78-81). Once I was happy with the fit of the ends, I glued only the center tenon in place so that the panel can move with fluctuations in humidity.

Installing the hinges

For aesthetic and practical reasons, I chose butt hinges for this chest. I left the top oversized until the hinges were installed; then I marked the overhang and cut it to its finished size. The back edge of the panel sits flush to the back of the chest, and its edges overhang the chest equally on both sides, a bit less in front.

Marking and mortising the carcase—The chest was mortised for the hinges first. I clamped a batten on the inside of the chest, level with the top edge to give the router base more stability. I set the router bit to cut slightly less than half the diameter of the hinge pin. This makes the back edge of the top sit slightly above the back edge of the chest and helps the front sit flat.

After routing the bulk of each mortise, I cleaned and squared the corners with a paring chisel. I used a steel screw to cut the threads and then drove in the brass screws that came with the hinges.

Marking and mortising the top—With the hinges attached to the chest, I brought the top next to the chest for marking the mortises in the top. Then I routed and pared them out, just as I did with

Slightly tapered plugs seat easily. *Wenge plugs are cut to length, planed to fit and then tapered so that they'll enter the squared screw holes easily. A dot of glue holds them in place.*

Plugs are easy to chamfer. *Chamfering all 40 plugs took less than an hour. Plastic laminate protects the chest when the author levers his chisel to pare the inner faces of the plugs.*

Clean styling and simple construction make this chest a versatile piece of furniture and a relatively quick project to build.

the chest. To check the fit of the top to the chest, I put one screw into each leaf of the top panel, which allowed me to adjust the hinges if necessary. Once I'd positioned the top on the chest just right, I marked the overhang, took the top off the chest and trimmed the top to size. Then I sanded it and refastened the hinges, adding the other two screws in each hinge leaf on the top.

Later I added a brass lid stay to keep the top from flopping open and pulling out the hinges. Several coats of shellac finished off the chest nicely, giving me a beautiful home for my old sweater. □

Gary Rogowski teaches woodworking and is a professional furnituremaker in Portland, Ore.

A Small Bureau Built to Last

Opaque finish and applied moldings cloak a flock of dovetails

by Robert Treanor

The dovetail joint's prevalence and persistence is due to its unsurpassed ability to hold pieces of wood together. The painted chest of drawers I made (see the photo at left) illustrates the strength and versatility of the dovetail in a variety of forms. Tapered sliding half-dovetails lock the top to the sides; half-blind dovetails join the sides to the bottom; sliding dovetails link the drawer dividers to the sides; and through- and half-blind dovetails join the drawers (see the drawings on pp. 82-83).

All this dovetailing makes the piece rock solid, but it is hidden strength. The chest has an unimposing scale that suits it to a living room, where it could stand at the end of a sofa and serve as an end table as well as a bureau. The moldings that hide its joinery are clean and simple, particularly the single-arch molding on the front of the chest with its bird's-mouth joints at the drawer dividers and its tapers, top and bottom.

Construction

I began the chest by gluing up material to form the top, bottom and sides. I used ash, a ring-porous, coarse-textured hardwood. Because I intended to paint the piece, I wasn't too careful about the color match of planks. But because the wood's coarse texture would show, I took pains to ensure figure and grain were consistent between the boards to be edge-glued.

A strong, self-locking joint—I used tapered, sliding half-dovetails to join the case sides to the top (see figure 1 on p. 82). This joint is excellent in a situation where one case member runs past or

overhangs another. Its advantages are many: It is self-locking, so it will hold both pieces rigid and flat even if the glue should fail; it won't bind in assembly; and it is strong. The half-dovetail is a variation on tapered sliding dovetails in which the pin seen in cross section has only one wedged side; the other side is simply a rabbet that tapers from one end of the joint to the other.

I made sockets for these pins in two stages. The first cut was a dado routed with a ⅜-in. straight bit along the tapered layout line. I routed the dado to a depth of ½ in. in several passes. With both dadoes cut, I changed to a ½-in. dovetail bit, set my scrap-stock fence parallel to the square layout line and routed the dovetail side of the socket in one pass (see the top photo).

I kept the dovetail bit at the same setting to cut the mating tapered half-dovetail pins on the tops of the case sides. I

locked the side in my bench vise and clamped a freshly milled piece of scrap along the top edge to give the router a greater bearing surface. Then, using the router's guide fence, I cut the dovetail along the outside face of the sides. Next I cut the tapered side of the half-dovetail with a rabbet plane. I clamped a fence along the shoulder line and guided the plane against it, as shown in the center photo. I planed down close to the taper line, taking light passes as I neared it. Before I reached the line, I started trial fitting the joint. This type of joint goes together sloppily until it's nearly home. The final inch or so will require firm hand pressure or even light mallet blows to close the joint completely. If you plane off too much, you can glue shims along the tapered edge and plane again to fit.

Tapered socket in two steps—First rout dadoes along the taper lines, as at right in the photo above. Then switch to a dovetail bit, clamp the fence parallel to the square layout line and cut the dovetailed side of the sockets, as at left in the photo above.

Sliding half-dovetails are finished with a rabbet plane (left). Cutting the taper of a sliding half-dovetail square with a rabbet plane instead of sloped on both sides like a full sliding dovetail makes a joint that's easier to fit. Stop and check the fit frequently as you approach the taper depth line.

Perfecting half-blind dovetails—After clearing waste with a Forstner bit in the drill press (below), the author pares to the lap line between pins of the half-blind dovetails at the bottom of the carcase sides. The board clamped to the workpiece guides the chisel for chopping through end grain.

Dovetails hide behind moldings and paint—This sofa-side chest of drawers (left) packs a robust array of joinery in a small frame.

Photos: Jonathan Binzen

Half-blind dovetails join the case sides to the bottom. I waited before cutting the bottom to length until I had the sides dry-fit to the top and could get an empirical measurement. I used nine tails across the width of the bottom, but the number or spacing isn't critical.

Because the pins on half-blind dovetails don't go through, it's harder to use them to lay out the tails, so I cut the tails first and lay out the pins from them. I do most of my dovetail sawing with Japanese dozuki saws, which are fast, accurate, easy to control and leave only a hairline kerf. After using the tails to lay out the pins in the sides, I cut and chop the remainder of the joint. I often hog out waste between the pins with a Forstner bit in the drill press. That makes the chisel work much lighter (see the bottom photo on p. 81). These joints won't show, but the more accurately they're cut the stronger the case will be and the closer the case will be to self-squaring. The joints will also provide practice, if needed, for the half-blind dovetails at the fronts of the drawers, the first place many people look when they open a drawer.

Dividers and tenons—The joinery for the drawer dividers at the front and back of the case and the runners between them is a hybrid. The dividers are attached to the sides with sliding dovetails, which keep the sides from bowing and the dividers in place. The runners are tongued along one edge and let into a dado in the cabinet side and are tenoned at each end into the drawer dividers (see figure 2).

I cut a ½-in.-wide dado ⅛ in. deep for each of the runners

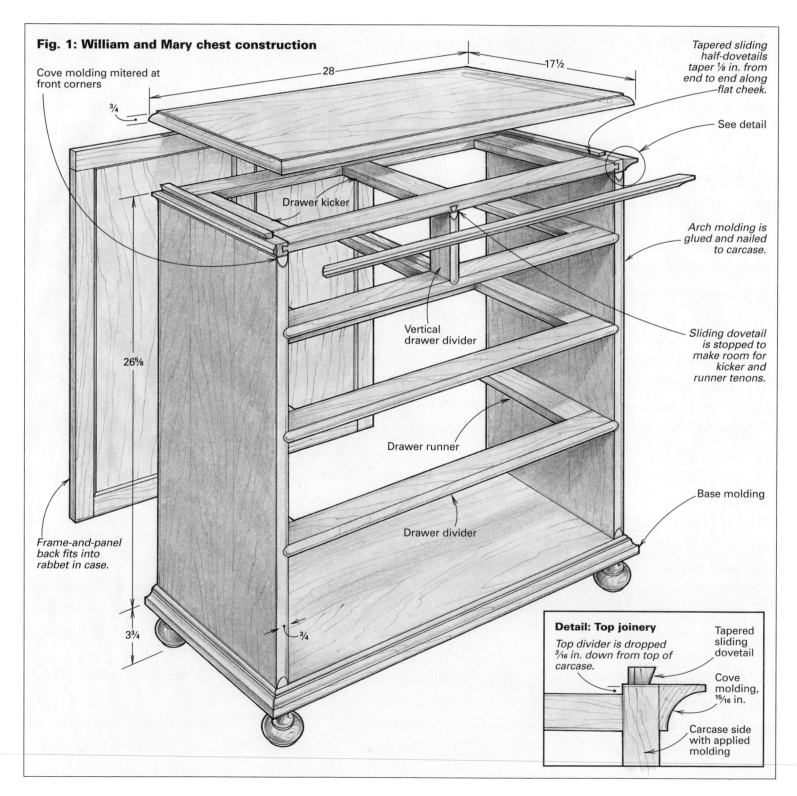

Fig. 1: William and Mary chest construction

Cove molding mitered at front corners

28

17½

¾

Tapered sliding half-dovetails taper ⅛ in. from end to end along flat cheek.

See detail

Drawer kicker

Arch molding is glued and nailed to carcase.

Vertical drawer divider

Sliding dovetail is stopped to make room for kicker and runner tenons.

26⅝

Drawer runner

Drawer divider

Base molding

Frame-and-panel back fits into rabbet in case.

3¾

¾

Detail: Top joinery

Top divider is dropped ³⁄₁₆ in. down from top of carcase.

Tapered sliding dovetail

Cove molding, ¹⁵⁄₁₆ in.

Carcase side with applied molding

Drawings: David Dann

and for the kickers above the top drawers. As well as housing the runners, the dadoes index the router jig I use to cut the sliding dovetail sockets for the dividers. The jig is a simple assembly: An indexing bar on its underside fits in the dado, arms guide the router and a center section both limits the router's travel and provides a place to attach the jig to the workpiece with drywall screws (see the center photo on p. 84). With the jig in place, I waste the bulk of the material with a ½-in. straight bit. Then the socket can be cut in one pass with a ¾-in. dovetail bit.

With the drawer dividers cut to length, scraped and sanded, I cut dovetails on their ends. I cut them on the router table with the same bit I used to cut their mating dovetail sockets. I clamp a high fence to the table to aid in keeping the pieces stable and run them past the bit vertically. The remaining joinery on the dividers are mortises cut at each end that will receive the tenons on the runners. I rout these with the dividers wedge-locked in a mortising box. I use a plunge router with a straight bit and cut in several passes. Then I square up the mortises by hand.

To fit the runners, I cut a ⅛-in. by ½-in. tongue on one edge and tenons on each end. When the case is assembled, I'll glue the tenons into the front dividers but will leave them dry at the back to allow for seasonal movement of the case. Be sure to leave a gap between the shoulder of the dry tenon and the back divider. The size of the gap will depend on what fluctuations of humidity the piece is likely to encounter.

Gluing up the case

The case is now nearly ready to glue up. But before that step, I shaped the edge of the top and routed rabbets in the parts to accept the frame-and-panel back. Because the joinery is all dovetails, I needed very few clamps. I used urea formaldehyde glue because it has a longer open time than the polyvinyl acetates (PVAs), and I planned to assemble the whole main case at once.

I began the assembly by applying glue to the tapered sliding half-dovetail sockets in the underside of the top. If the joint is a tight fit, only a small amount of glue is needed. I carefully slid the joint together, tapping lightly as needed. With the sides joined to the top, I turned the case upside down and glued the bottom to the sides, knocking the joints home evenly with a mallet and a block of scrap. Then I checked for square and cleaned off glue squeeze-out. If necessary, I use bar clamps to square up the case and hold things in alignment as the assembly continues.

I glued in the front dividers next, using glue judiciously and checking for square after each divider was glued in. Then I flipped the case over, so it sat on its front face. I applied glue to the mortises in the front dividers and installed the runners into the mortises and the dadoes cut into the sides, taking care not to get any glue in the dadoes. Finally, I glued the back dividers into their dovetail slots, pinching myself to refrain

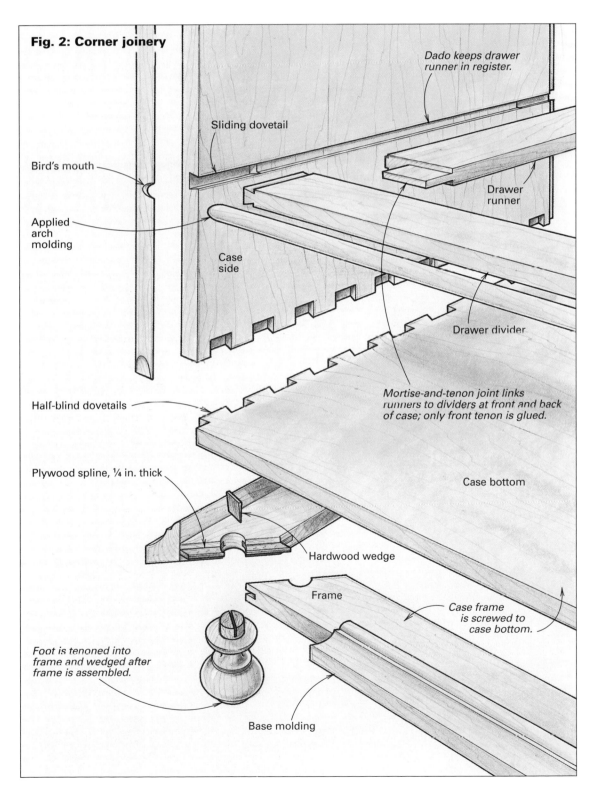

Fig. 2: Corner joinery

Bird's mouth

Applied arch molding

Sliding dovetail

Case side

Dado keeps drawer runner in register.

Drawer runner

Half-blind dovetails

Plywood spline, ¼ in. thick

Drawer divider

Mortise-and-tenon joint links runners to dividers at front and back of case; only front tenon is glued.

Hardwood wedge

Case bottom

Foot is tenoned into frame and wedged after frame is assembled.

Frame

Case frame is screwed to case bottom.

Base molding

from gluing the mortise-and-tenon joint that attaches them to the runners.

Dressing the case

To make the arch molding that covers the front edges of the case, I milled a straight-grained board to ¾ in. thick. I cut the profile on a router table with a fingernail or half-radius bit. The entire edge is shaped, so I put several layers of masking tape along the out-feed side of the fence to create an offset bearing surface. I ripped the molded edges off the board with the tablesaw.

I applied the arch molding after the cove molding at the top of the case was already in place. Fitting the small bird's-mouth junctions of the arch moldings requires patience and sharp tools. I began by

cutting the vertical pieces of molding to length and taping them to the front edge of the sides. Then I carefully marked the locations of the drawer dividers on the moldings, removed the moldings and laid out the bird's mouths on their back faces. I cut the waste away with a fine toothed backsaw and cleaned the cut by paring the remaining material with a sharp chisel, working up to the line with light cuts. Then I taped the moldings back onto the case and

took measurements for horizontal moldings. I cut the horizontal moldings to length with a backsaw and a miter box. I glued and nailed the moldings to the case after all the joints had been fitted. I scarfed the ends of the moldings to meet the cove molding at the top of the case and the frame molding at the bottom. It's a small detail, but one that gives the piece its feeling of simple refinement. I made the cut by eye with a chisel, as shown in the bottom photo.

*A **painted finish*** is in keeping with the early 18th-century origins of this chest of drawers. I like the finish for the bold field of color it provides from afar and for the way it emphasizes the texture of the wood when seen up close. I used Fancy Chair Green, a latex finish that simulates milk paint (it is one of the Williamsburg Paint Colors made by the Stulb Co.; I bought mine from Primrose Distributing, 54445 Rose Road, South Bend, Ind. 46628; 219-234-6728). To prepare for painting, I wet down the surface with a damp rag to raise the grain. When the case was dry, I scuff-sanded the whiskers that had been raised. On the drawers, I put strips of painter's masking tape just behind the lap of the half-blind dovetails, creating the detail shown in the far left photo. I applied the paint with a natural bristle brush directly to the bare wood. I skipped a primer coat because I wanted to avoid filling the grain. I let the first coat dry overnight and rubbed down the surface with 0000 steel wool. When a second coat had dried completely, I finished the case with a coat of satin varnish to make the color richer and to give the surface more depth. I finished the drawers and the inside of the case with three coats of a thinned shellac. Shellac cannot be used as a topcoat on the painted surfaces because it tends to lift the paint. With the finish completely dry, I mounted the period brass pulls (available from Horton Brasses, P.O. Box 120, Dept. F, Cromwell, Conn. 06416; 203-635-4400), glued and wedged the feet to the base frame, and screwed the base frame to the case. □

Paint pronounces the texture—On a coarse-textured wood like ash, an opaque finish brings out the grain while hiding the color (above). The author left the ash case and drawer fronts unprimed to keep from filling the pores. He used painter's tape to mask the drawer sides and drawer openings. The interior finish is shellac.

A good jig is easy to locate (right). The drawer-runner dadoes across the case sides double as an indexing slot for the simple router jig, which cuts the stopped sliding dovetail sockets for the drawer dividers.

Scarfs cut by eye—A few mallet taps produce the scarf detail at the ends of the vertical arch moldings (below). The author keeps his first scarf in view and approximates the angle on the other cuts.

Robert Treanor, a former teacher in the woodworking program at San Francisco State University, builds and writes about furniture in the Bay area.

Aligning the front on a chest of drawers—The author has developed a technique for beltsanding his cabinet fronts and drawers at the same time. When he combines them with front-mounted stops, the cabinet faces are flat and smooth and drawers always align with the face frame, regardless of season.

Drawer Fronts That Fit Flush

Beltsanding and drawer stops leave a front that's always aligned

by Christian H. Becksvoort

From *Fine Woodworking* (January 1994) 104:82-84

Maintaining drawer-front alignment to the face frame can be a seasonal problem on furniture built with slab (or wide board) construction and typical rear-mounted drawer stops. The depth of the case can vary considerably from summer to winter depending upon the width, species and cut of the wood (see *FWW* #94, pp. 38-41). The length of wood does not change noticeably with changes in moisture content, however, so flush-mounted drawers with stops at the back tend to protrude in the winter and are recessed in the summer.

I've borrowed a technique of front-mounted drawer stops from an antique piece and have used it quite successfully for the last several years. Front-stopped drawers always maintain the same position in relation to the front of the cabinet, and they don't need to be individually adjusted for each drawer. This technique uses a stop glued to the divider under the drawer instead of placing the stop at the back of the drawer.

The stops also help me sand the drawer fronts and cabinet front at the same time, ensuring a flat, smooth plane and perfect drawer alignment. I install the drawers in the carcase against the stops and wedge them in place. I then beltsand the entire front of the case, including drawer fronts, drawer dividers and the front edges of the cabinet sides, as shown in the bottom photo on p. 87. The drawers support the belt sander, so I don't have to worry about balancing it on the thin dividers and gouging the case sides when I sand to the edge of the case. While sanding the drawer fronts, I'm also able to sand out all the minor misalignment that occurs when sliding the dovetailed dividers into place in the case sides.

There is no other technique that will leave the case and drawers as flat and as perfectly aligned. The whole system works because I house my drawer bottoms in grooves that are $\frac{5}{16}$ in. from the bottom edge of the drawers. This leaves plenty of clearance for the $\frac{1}{4}$-in.-thick drawer stops glued to the drawer divider below the drawer. The stops are out of sight and don't interfere with the drawer's contents as top-mounted stops might.

Fitting the stops

First I fit the drawers, leaving about $\frac{1}{32}$-in. to $\frac{3}{64}$-in. gap on either side, and a gap above the drawer appropriate to the size, species and moisture content of the drawer front. I also make the drawers short enough (about $\frac{1}{2}$-in. shy of the full cabinet depth) to accommodate more than the full range of movement expected in the cabinet side.

Then I mark the location of the stops, referencing from the back of the case. If this were a perfect world, I could simply mark from the front of the case, allowing for the thickness of the drawer front and the leather bumper. But perfectly aligning the snug, sliding dovetail joints that connect the dividers to the carcase is not an easy task. Sometimes the glue grabs before the divider is fully seated; other times that last tap knocks the divider $\frac{1}{16}$ in. past where you want it, and no amount of pounding will reverse it. Referencing the stops from the back of the case lets me sand out misalignments when I'm sanding the drawer fronts to align with the case.

To make sure that all the stops are aligned, first I find the divider that is inset the farthest. I measure from the front of this divider, deducting the thickness of the drawer front plus a leather bumper. This mark is where the front of the stop needs to be to leave the drawer front flush with the divider's face. I then make a gauge for marking the rest of the dividers by measuring from the back of the cabinet to the mark. I cut a 4-in.- to 6-in.-wide scrap board to that length to serve as a guide for laying out all the stops. The gauge is slipped into the opening, making sure it is pushed tightly against the cabinet back and side, so all the drawers will be equidistant from the back of the cabinet. The stop position is marked by scrib-

Scribed lines accurately position stops—The author uses a 4-in.- to 6-in.-wide board, cut to the appropriate length, as a gauge to scribe alignment marks for the drawer stops. Measuring from the cabinet back eliminates any variations that may have occurred when gluing in the dovetailed drawer dividers.

The drawer stops are glued, positioned on the dividers and held in place with spring clamps. The stops must be thin enough to clear the drawer bottoms and short enough to allow drawer side clearance at the ends. Leather bumpers are temporarily glued to the stops to position the drawers for sanding.

ing a line along the front edge of the measuring gauge, as shown in the top photo. I find that a knife-scribed line is more accurate than a pencil line when marking the stops. To make the scribed line more visible, you can darken it by running a pencil sharpened to a chisel point along the line.

I cut the stops from waste stock, $\frac{3}{8}$ in. to $\frac{1}{2}$ in. wide and $\frac{1}{4}$ in. thick. For drawers 14 in. and narrower, I usually use a single strip across the divider. The strips are centered in the drawer opening, and they leave plenty of room on each side for the $\frac{1}{2}$-in.-thick drawer sides. Wider drawers get two stops about 2 in. to 3 in. long. After sanding, the stops are glued to the scribed lines and held in place with spring clamps (see the bottom photo above). The stops must be located about 1 in. from the carcase sides so they don't interfere with the drawer sides. Then the leather bumpers are temporarily glued to the fronts of the stops, using a minute amount of glue. After the front has been sanded, the leather is removed for finishing (otherwise it becomes hard) and reapplied when the case is complete. I prefer the quality feel and sound of leather bumpers on a custom piece because they make a better impression than the rubber, plastic or cork bumpers so frequently found on store-bought furniture.

Sanding the case and drawers

The first time I used this method of stopping drawers, it dawned on me that this was the perfect solution to sanding the entire cab-

Wedging the drawers in place holds them for beltsanding. The drawers should be wedged on each side to center them in the opening and wedged at the top to hold them firmly against the drawer dividers and stops. The entire front of the cabinet can then be sanded to one flat, smooth plane.

Sanding the cabinet front, with the drawers held in place by front-mounted stops and wedges, ensures that the entire face of the cabinet will be flat and smooth. The drawers support the sander and prevent gouging the face frame. This technique eliminates the need to set each drawer individually.

inet face. No more balancing a belt sander on a ¾-in.-wide divider, hoping not to gouge the cabinet side or intersecting dividers. This was a real bonus. It takes a little preparation, but the results are well worth the effort.

First, after drilling holes for hardware or knobs in the drawer fronts, I slide all the drawers back into the case. Next I make shims, using ¹⁄₁₆-in. by ½-in. pine strips, tapering the ends into wedges with a quick knife cut. I shim the drawer sides to center the drawer from side to side in the opening, as shown in the top photo on this page. Then, using thicker pine strips, I shim the top of the drawer front to hold the drawer against the divider below it. The shims should be good and tight to keep the drawer from vibrating during the sanding process.

With all the drawers securely in place, I lay the cabinet on its back on two padded sawhorses of convenient height. Using a belt sander and an 80-grit belt, I work my way across the face of the cabinet, from one end to the other, as shown in the bottom photo on this page. Before sanding with a 120-grit belt, I check the cabinet face for high and low spots by laying a 5-ft.-long straightedge on the face of the cabinet and sighting along the straightedge's bottom edge. I repeat the process in four or five places across the cabinet face, marking the high spots with a pencil line. I then connect these marks, making a topographical map, of sorts, on the cabinet face to show me where more material needs to be removed. After sanding with 120-grit and 150-grit belts, I switch to a vibrating-pad sander or random-orbit sander and 180-grit, 220-grit and 320-grit discs.

Finishing details

At this point, the front of the cabinet is a single, flat, smooth plane. I remove the drawers for a final hand-sanding with a bolt through the knob hole. The first drawer is always difficult to remove, especially if the shimming was done correctly and you forgot to drill the knob holes before wedging in the drawers. However, once the first one is out, I have room to reach in and push out the rest from behind. I hand-sand each drawer face with 400-grit paper and ease and smooth all the edges. The same goes for the cabinet face: Remove all traces of cross-grain scratches and break all edges. Then vacuum out the inside of the case, remove the leather bumpers and the case is ready for the finish of your choice. □

Christian H. Becksvoort builds custom furniture in New Gloucester, Maine, and is a contributing editor to Fine Woodworking.

Curvaceous Carcase Construction

Slats dress up bendable-plywood sides

by John Eric Byers

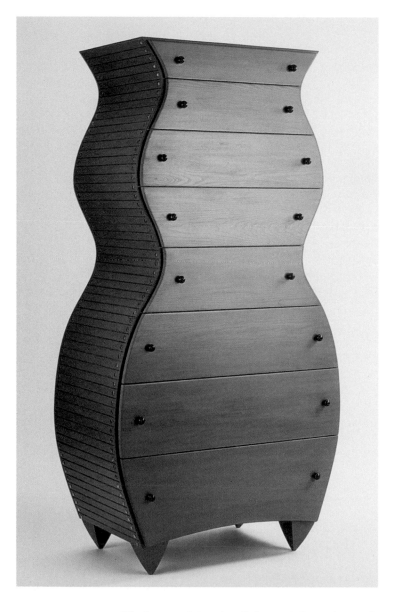

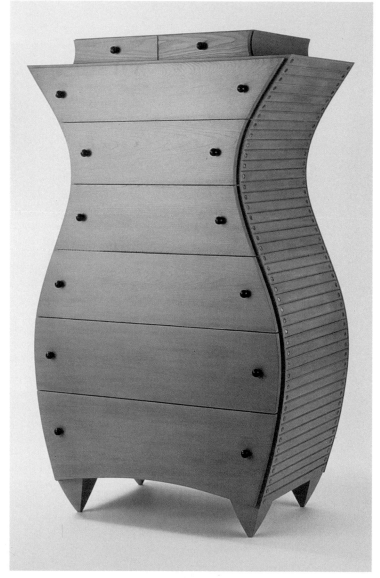

Thelma and Louise (*above left and right*) owe their shapely figures to the author's method for building curved-sided carcases. Byers applies layers of bending plywood over an inner plywood structure; then he covers the curved sides with decorative slats.

Byers' bending-plywood carcase construction lends itself to a wide range of furniture, including Temptation Chest, the ebonized-oak blanket chest shown at right.

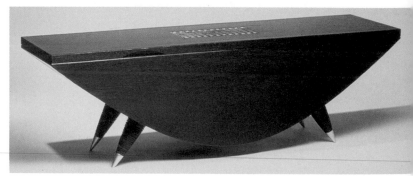

Photos this page: Thomas Brummett; drawing: Vince Babak

Turned, curvy forms have always influenced my work. My first lathe-turned-wood forms emulated fine glass and ceramic vessels. However, I found turning to be too limiting in terms of the kinds of objects I wanted to create, so I attended the Wendell Castle School to learn furnituremaking. After leaving school, I developed a construction technique to produce curved forms on a large scale. Pieces like *Thelma and Louise*, the two chests of drawers shown on the facing page, allow me to create functional furniture with voluptuous curves that invite interaction and have a strong physical, even anthropomorphic presence. I like to think that when I hear a noise downstairs at night, it might be one of my furniture pieces dancing around.

Besides allowing me to create the kinds of pieces I like, my curved carcase construction, as illustrated in the drawing, is really quite simple: An internal frame of plywood dividers provides housings for drawers and an armature for two layers of bending plywood, which make up the curved sides. After I add a plywood back and laminated strips on the curved edges, I dress up the bent sides with tambour-like slats. Finally, I build standard, box-like drawers with solid-wood drawer fronts with their ends sawn to match the curvature of the piece. This way, the drawers don't have to be made to fit curved, irregular spaces. Usually, the width of the drawer varies to suit the space between the curves, but these standard, box-like drawers are as easy and quick to make for any standard, rectangular carcase.

My construction method is very flexible, so I can create many different types of curved-sided furniture pieces besides chests of drawers, such as small cabinets, night tables and the blanket chest shown in the bottom photo on the facing page. These pieces employ some variations, such as hinged doors on one of my cabinets and the solid-wood front, back and lift-up lid on the blanket chest.

Designing a curvy carcase

I view the design of my furniture pieces as basically a subtractive process; I draw a square and "carve" away the negative space until I end up with a form that looks right. I start with gesture drawing, small thumbnail sketches that allow me to try out different ideas on paper. Then I turn a promising sketch into a full-scale elevation on a sheet of 1/8-in. door-skin plywood. With symmetrical carcases, I refine the curve on one half of the elevation, cut out this half profile and use it as a template to draw both halves of the case. This full-size drawing helps me visualize the final form of the piece. I draw the position of all plywood dividers that will separate and contain the drawers and work out the scheme of how tall and wide the drawers will be in the irregular spaces as I go along. Because each irregularly shaped drawer front will attach to a standard drawer, I can make the drawers different dimensions to keep things interesting and still end up with drawers that are standard construction.

The ends of the inner frame's horizontal dividers (the equivalent of dust panels) provide points of attachment for the plywood skin that will be bent over them. Therefore, I miter these ends, as well as the ends of the top and bottom panels, to best contact the curved plywood. I measure these angles directly from the full-size drawing with a bevel gauge. After cutting out and mitering the panels, I apply a 3/8-in.-thick edgeband to the front of each and sand the surfaces. Next, I cut the vertical dividers to create the rectangular boxes that contain the drawers. Then I glue and screw (sometimes I use biscuit joinery instead) the panels together to assemble the inner frame.

To make the surface of the curved sides, I apply the 3/8-in. bending plywood, which consists of three plys; two thicker outside plys with their grain running parallel and a thinner inside ply that runs perpendicular to the other two. Two layers of this flexible ply-

wood, which is sold by lumber dealers under many names including "wacky wood," are bent onto each carcase side. After cutting two pieces to size for each carcase side, I simply bend the first layer directly over the horizontal dividers and screw it into their ends. As I work around the carcase side, I adjust the curvature of the bending plywood before screwing it to each divider to get a smooth curve and avoid flat spots. A second layer of bending ply is glued on over the first layer, initially held with spring-action clamps and then screwed and nailed in place. Pneumatically driven 3/4-in. or 5/8-in.-long brads, liberally applied over the surface (as shown in the top photo on the following page), ensure that the two plywood layers will glue tightly together without voids, mak-

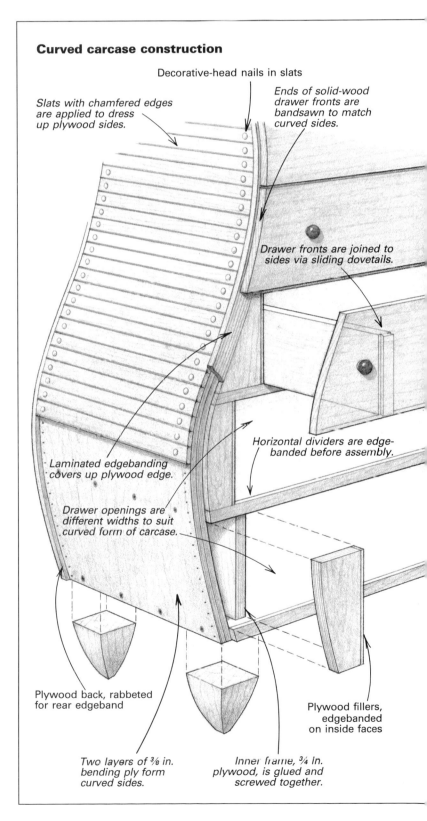

Curved carcase construction

Decorative-head nails in slats

Slats with chamfered edges are applied to dress up plywood sides.

Ends of solid-wood drawer fronts are bandsawn to match curved sides.

Drawer fronts are joined to sides via sliding dovetails.

Horizontal dividers are edge-banded before assembly.

Laminated edgebanding covers up plywood edge.

Drawer openings are different widths to suit curved form of carcase.

Plywood back, rabbeted for rear edgeband

Plywood fillers, edgebanded on inside faces

Two layers of 3/8 in. bending ply form curved sides.

Inner frame, 3/4 in. plywood, is glued and screwed together.

From *Fine Woodworking* (July 1992) 95:64-66

The author glues and nails a second layer of thin bending plywood over the first, which was screwed to the end of each divider as the ply was bent into place. Byers uses spring clamps temporarily to keep the ply in place while a pneumatic nail gun drives dozens of brads to secure the layer.

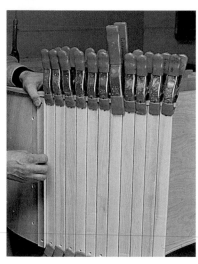

Solid-wood edgebanding that's laminated together from thin strips covers the edges of the bent-plywood carcase. The carcase itself acts as the bending form, and spring clamps hold the glued laminae in place.

Chamfered slats, glued and nailed over bent sides, provide a decorative covering for the carcase. A strip of scrap plastic laminate acts as a spacer to allow room for solid-wood slats to expand and contract.

ing the curved sides strong. For very tight curved sides, I apply a few curved plywood ribs between dividers on the inner carcase to help fair out the tight bend.

Laminated edgebanding

After the sides are glued, screwed and nailed on, I use a rabbet plane to trim both front and back edges of the plywood in preparation for an edgeband that finishes off these sides. Many 1/16-in.-thick strips of hardwood laminated together comprise this band. On the front of the piece, this strip is formed directly to the front edge of the carcase. I use enough strips to make the edgeband about 1 1/8 wide. This thickness equals two bending plys (3/4 in.) plus 3/8 in., which is the thickness of the slats that will cover the sides. A few scraps of plywood temporarily nailed to the inside surfaces of the bent sides provide the form for the edgeband as it's clamped in place with spring-action clamps (as shown in the center photo). Tape masks the edge of the side, so the strip won't stick to it as the laminae are glued together. After the laminated strip dries, I scrape off the excess adhesive and glue it in place on the edge after removing the tape.

At the rear of the carcase, a 1/2-in. plywood back is cut out and glued and screwed onto the inner frame and curved sides. The back is flush trimmed all around, and the curved edges are rabbeted about 3/8 in. deep and 1 1/8 in. wide. A rear edgeband is then laminated and glued into this rabbet—same as the front edgeband.

Gluing on the slats

The individual slats that cover up the bending ply and dress up the curved carcase sides are machined and applied next. After they're thickness planed to 3/8 in. thick and ripped to 1 1/2 in. wide, I chamfer all the edges and ends on one side of each slat with a 45° bit in my router. Then I apply the slats, gluing them on with yellow glue and using spring clamps to anchor them while the glue dries. In cases where the carcase will be painted, I nail the slats on with the brad gun and fill the holes with putty. The brad holes are also covered by decorative-head nails. To ensure that the solid-wood slats have room to expand and contract, I leave a slight gap between adjacent slats. I set the gap by using a scrap of plastic countertop laminate as a spacer (see the bottom photo on this page). Once all the slats have been mounted, I drive two decorative-head nails into each slat. I do this as much for the dressy effect as for strength. The nails I use most often are made of copper and several styles are available from Faering Design Inc., Route 1, PO Box 223, Sutton's Bay, Mich. 49682; (616) 271-6729. To complete the casework, I cut and edgeband the plywood fillers to fit the irregular spaces between the drawer housings and the curved sides and glue and screw them in place. Also, I veneer the plywood top.

I build the drawers with solid-wood sides and 1/4 in. plywood bottoms. Using standard construction, I join the sides to the back with through-dovetails. A groove near the bottom edge of the sides and back houses the drawer bottom. The drawer faces are ripped to width from solid-wood stock, and the ends are bandsawn to match the side curvatures. I attach the fronts to the drawer sides with sliding dovetails made with the router.

Sometimes a case's design creates built-in feet for the piece, but I often add shaped or turned feet, as on my blanket chest, or bandsawn feet, as I used on *Thelma and Louise* (see the photos on p. 88). I use a variety of finishes, including clear lacquer and pickled finishes, but most often I finish my work with milk paints. The colorful finish further enhances the animated quality of my pieces. □

John Eric Byers is a furniture designer/craftsman who works in Philadelphia, Pa.

Photos this page: Sandor Nagyszalanczy

A Cherry Clothes Tree

A simple project to hang your hat on

by Christian H. Becksvoort

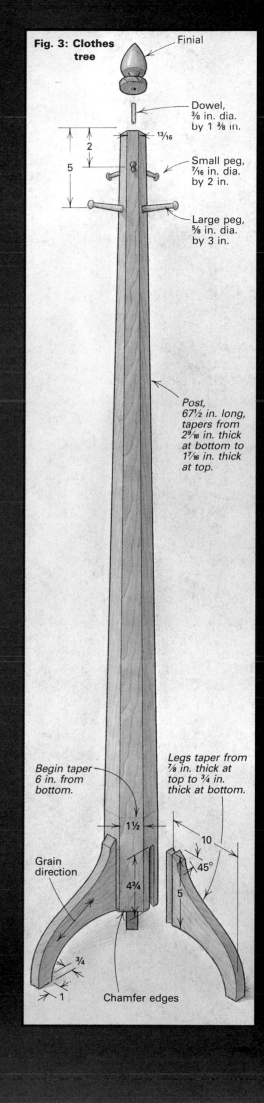

Fig. 1: Finial

Finial is 3¾ in. high.

1⅞ in. dia.

1¾ in. dia.

1²¹⁄₃₂ in. dia.

Carve or file facets to match top of post.

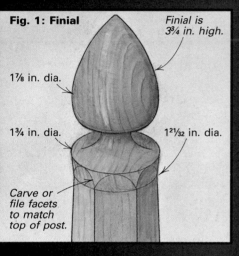

Fig. 2: Section view of post and legs

¾

⅝

⅞

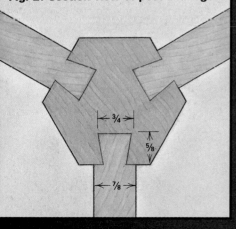

The author borrowed design details from a number of pieces to create this cherry clothes tree. The legs are from a Shaker round stand, the post and finial from a pencil-post bed and the pegs from a Shaker pegged wall board.

Fig. 3: Clothes tree

Finial

Dowel, ⅜ in. dia. by 1 ⅜ in.

13⁄16

2

5

Small peg, 7⁄16 in. dia. by 2 in.

Large peg, ⅝ in. dia. by 3 in.

Post, 67½ in. long, tapers from 2⁹⁄16 in. thick at bottom to 1⁷⁄16 in. thick at top.

Begin taper 6 in. from bottom.

Legs taper from ⅞ in. thick at top to ¾ in. thick at bottom.

1½

10

45°

Grain direction

4¾

5

¾

1

Chamfer edges

Recently I was commissioned to build a bedroom clothes tree to complement a cherry pencil-post bed I had already made (*FWW #76*, pp. 32-37). My initial reaction was to copy the bed's eight-sided posts. An eight-sided clothes-tree post with four legs seemed logical, but no matter what kind of legs I drew, none looked right. I even considered gluing up a lathe-turned flattened cone for a base, but this was too heavy visually.

To lighten the appearance and conform to the simple lines of the bed, I decided on a tapered hexagonal post with three legs secured with sliding dovetails. I made full-size cardboard cutouts so I could determine the best shape for the legs, and settled on the cyma legs, one of my favorite styles, taken from a Shaker round stand. Shaker pegs were a logical choice for hangers. I used three 3-in.-long pegs on the same facets as the legs and three 2-in.-long pegs higher up on the remaining three facets. To top off the post, I used the same modified acorn finial as the one on the pencil-post bed. This finial design was originally used to top off the back legs on chairs by Robert Wagan of the Mt. Lebanon Shaker community in New York.

Making the post—To build the clothes tree, I started by first ripping the post stock into a hexagon with 1½-in.-wide facets and then tapering it on my jointer. To prepare the stock, crosscut a 3½-in.-wide piece of ¹²⁄₄ cherry to 67½ in. long. Joint the wide face of the stock flat and plane it to 2⁹⁄₁₆ in. thick. The 1½-in.-wide facets at the base of the post predetermine the measurements: 2⁹⁄₁₆ in. from face to face and 2¹⁵⁄₁₆ in. from point to point (see figure 4). To lay out the hexagon, I divided the thickness of the stock in half and scribed a centerline across the bottom. Using a sliding T-bevel set at 120°, I drew the lines shown in figure 4 to define the first two cuts.

Before ripping the bevels on the tablesaw, move the fence to the side of the blade opposite the direction the blade tilts, raise the blade about 1½ in. and then set it to 30°. Adjust the fence, as shown in figure 4, so the blade cuts on the waste side of the layout line and the cut-off scrap is not trapped between the fence and the blade. After making the first cut, I flipped the stock end for end, keeping the same edge against the fence, and ripped the second facet. Since I didn't change the fence position, both cuts met at the centerline. Now, on both faces of the stock, draw a pencil mark 1½ in. from the cuts just made and, using the sliding T-bevel, draw the lines on the end of the stock for the third and fourth cuts. As you did for the first two cuts, adjust the fence and make the third cut, and then flip the stock end for end and rip the last bevel.

I prefer tapering the post on the jointer because it's quick, easy and produces smooth surfaces. You want to leave 6 in. of untapered stock at the bottom of the post, for dovetailing the legs, and then taper the remainder from 2⁹⁄₁₆ in. thick to 1⁷⁄₁₆ in. thick at the top. This requires removing ⁹⁄₁₆ in. from each facet, which I do in two passes with the jointer set to take a ⁹⁄₃₂-in.-deep cut. First, draw a reference line at 30¾ in. from the top on each facet. Then with the top of the post at the end of the infeed table, lower the reference mark onto the cutter and feed the post, bottom end first, through the cutter. If your jointer doesn't have this capacity, make multiple passes of lighter cuts, but taper each facet equally. Tapering can also be done with a bandsaw and handplane, but this is difficult because the bandsaw table must be tilted to 30°. When you are finished tapering, sand out planer marks or sawmarks, easing the transition between the taper and the straight surface at the base. (See *FWW #54*, p. 54, for more on tapering on a jointer.) A word of advice regardless of your tapering method: Mark the tapers before cutting them and draw the smaller hexagon, ¹³⁄₁₆ in. per side, on the top of the post. As the tapering progresses, the end view becomes an optical illusion, and without these marks, it is difficult to determine which facets have been tapered.

Shaping and dovetailing the legs—The three legs that support the clothes tree are cut from ⅞-in.-thick stock, with the grain running the length of the leg, and dovetailed into the post. Develop a pattern from figure 3 and then trace it onto the stock and bandsaw the three legs. Be sure that the bottom of the leg and the edge that will be dovetailed into the post are perpendicular and that this edge is perfectly straight. I used a drum sander attachment on my lathe to sand the curve underneath the leg flat and to shape the curve on the top to a crowned profile.

When the three legs are sanded, it's time to cut the dovetails, which can be done on a table-mounted router or by hand. Using a router-table setup is less time-consuming, but not as much fun. I'll discuss both methods, since I use both in different circumstances.

To rout sockets and pins for sliding dovetails, I use a ¾-in. dovetail bit with a 14° angle chucked in my table-mounted router. Set the bit for a ⅝-in.-deep cut and adjust the fence so the cutter is centered on a facet of the post laying flat on the table. I clamp a second fence of scrapwood on the other side of the post to hold it in place, and then clamp a stop to the fence 4 in. past the router bit to control these cuts. Hold the post firmly down on the table

Fig. 4: Laying out and cutting the hexagonal post

Cherry, 2⁹⁄₁₆x3½x67½

Saw fence

Third cut

Second cut

Saw fence

2¹⁵⁄₁₆

Sawblade

Centerline

First cut

Last cut

30°

Saw table

1½

Above: Fences on two sides of the post and a stop block to control the length of cut ensure accurate and consistent dovetail slots for joining the legs to the post.

Right: Becksvoort cuts the dovetail pins on the leg ends quickly after setting the fence through a series of trial-and-error tests on a scrap block.

Photo previous page: Kip Brundage; drawings: Vince Babak

Using the dovetail pin on the leg as a guide, the author scribes the layout for the slot, which is cut with a dovetail saw and then chopped with chisels.

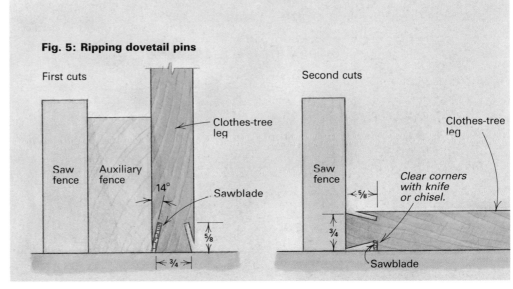

Fig. 5: Ripping dovetail pins

First cuts

Saw fence

Auxiliary fence

14°

Clothes-tree leg

Sawblade

⅝

¾

Second cuts

Saw fence

⅝

¾

Clothes-tree leg

Clear corners with knife or chisel.

Sawblade

and slide it into the cutter, as shown in the top photo on the facing page, until it hits the stop. Gently back out the post and repeat this twice more on the alternate facets until you've cut 4¾-in.-long dovetail sockets for the three legs.

To cut matching pins on the legs, remove the stop and the second fence without changing the cutter height. Add a wooden auxiliary face to the fence and move this face into the cutter until a little less than ⅛ in. of the cutter is exposed. Then make a test run: slide a scrap block past the cutter, flip it over, cut the other side and fit it into one of the sockets. If the fit is too tight, move the fence back a hair and recut a scrap. If the fit is too loose, move the fence into the cutter and test again with another scrap. Once you've found the correct position for the fence, cut the pins on the three legs, as shown in the bottom right photo on the facing page.

If I'm not routing the dovetails, I usually rip the pins on the leg first and then handsaw or chisel the slots to fit. To do this, begin by setting the tablesaw blade to between 12° and 14°, so that it's just under ⅝ in. high, and by adjusting the fence to cut a pin about ¾ in. wide (see figure 5). Cut both sides of the pins on all three legs. Then reset the blade to 90°, lower it and cut the waste on the shoulders. The two sawcuts should just meet, but not overlap. The remaining waste in the corner must be cleaned out with a knife or chisel.

To lay out the dovetail slot, position the leg so that the pin rests on the bottom of the post, centered on one of the facets, with its shoulders touching the edge of the post. Mark around the pin with a knife, as shown in the photo above, and use a square to transfer these lines 4¾ in. down the face of the facet. With a dovetail saw, cut the slot on the waste side of the lines, being careful not to saw beyond the 4¾-in. stopping mark.

Clearing the waste from the slot takes about 30 minutes, if the grain is straight. First, anchor the post firmly in a vise with padding so it won't be marred. Then make a stop cut with a ½-in. chisel in the end of the slot. Next, waste the bulk of material from the post, beginning at the bottom and working to the stopped cut. To clean the bottom and sides to fit, use a no. 2 pencil and blacken the first ½ in. of the bottom and two sides of the pin. Force the pin into the slot until it binds and then withdraw it. The pencil smudges in the slot reveal tight areas where binding occurs. Shave these areas and slightly beyond with sharp ½-in., ⅝-in. and ¾-in. paring chisels. The pin slides about 1⁄16 in. to ⅛ in. further into the slot with each fitting. Continue the trial-and-trim technique until the pin hits the end of the slot. Although the fit must be tight, hand pressure should be enough to slide the leg into place. However, it may take a few mallet taps to get the leg out. Because each leg will fit slightly differently, I marked the slot and leg so they could be paired again during assembly.

When all the legs were fitted, I handsawed the flat area on top of

each leg to approximately 45°. Taper the leg from its ⅞-in. thickness at the dovetail to ¾ in. at the bottom of the foot. Now finish-sand all three legs and glue them into their respective slots. Because of this tight fit and the self-wedging action of the dovetails, clamping should not be necessary. When the glue has dried, sand the bottom sides of the three legs flush with the post.

Making and installing the pegs and finial—Although I turned the pegs for my clothes tree on a lathe, similar-size cherry pegs are available from Shaker Workshops (Box 1028, Concord, Mass. 01742; 617-646-8985) or Cherry Tree Toys, Inc. (Box 369, Belmont, Ohio 43718; 614-484-4363). Be sure you buy the pegs before drilling the post so the holes are the right size. My large pegs, located 5 in. from the top on the same facets as the legs, have ½-in.-dia. tenons, while the small ones, located 2 in. from the top on the remaining three facets, have ⅜-in.-dia. tenons. Lay out the holes on the centerline of each facet, and then tilt the table on the drill press to compensate for the taper of the post so that the facet lies perpendicular to the drill bit. Position the post under the bit and clamp it into place. Drill the ½-in. holes about ⅝ in. deep and the ⅜-in. holes ½ in. deep. I've found that the top hole for mounting the finial is best drilled with a doweling jig. To do this, find the center of the top and locate the barrel of the jig directly over the center. This is easiest if you insert a ⅜-in.-dia. brad-point bit into the barrel. Because the post is tapered, small shims are required at the top to mount the doweling jig.

To turn the pegs on the lathe, cut the tenons with a plug cutter on the drill press, and then mount the blank in a chuck, steadying it with the tailstock center. After you turn the pegs, cut off the waste, back off the tailstock center and finish-sand the pegs on the lathe. Apply a dab of glue to each tenon and glue the pegs into their holes.

The 1⅞-in.-dia. by 3¾-in.-long finial is turned from a 2x2x5 cherry blank. Before mounting the blank on the lathe, drill a ⅜-in.-dia. by ¾-in.-deep hole in the bottom of the finial for doweling it on the post. The finial flares slightly as it goes up from its base, which should be the same diameter as the corner-to-corner measurement at the top of the post. After the finial is turned, glue a ⅜-in.-dia. by 1⅜-in.-long dowel into the top of the post. Position the finial on the dowel and with a knife, outline the top of the post on the bottom of the finial. Carve or file six flat, half-oval facets into the base of the finial, as shown in figure 1. This provides a smooth transition from the turned finial to the hexagonal post. When the fit is perfect, sand the finial smooth, glue it to the post and apply the finish of your choice. I like the soft glow of a hand-rubbed oil finish. ☐

Christian H. Becksvoort builds custom furniture in New Gloucester, Maine, and is a contributing editor to FWW.

Making an End Table

The beauty of this Arts-and-Crafts design is in the details

by Stephen Lamont

Beauty that's more than skin deep. *This end table is solidly constructed and meticulously detailed. It should last generations.*

About 10 years ago, I began to tire of my job as a corporate pilot. The work was challenging and enjoyable, but the time away from home put a strain on my family. The job was becoming more technical, too. Temperamentally, I've always been more of a craftsman than a technician.

After considerable soul-searching, I decided to become a furnituremaker. I wanted a solid foundation of basic skills, so I went to England where I trained with Chris Faulkner. He emphasized developing hand-tool skills and building simple, comfortable furniture that asked to be used—a basic tenet of the British Arts-and-Crafts movement. My preferences to this day are for this kind of furniture and for the use of hand tools whenever their use will make a difference.

About two years ago, I designed and built the end table shown in the photo at left. Although it's an original design, many details come from other pieces of furniture in the British Arts-and-Crafts tradition. The joinery is mortise-and-tenon and dovetail throughout.

The construction of the table can be divided into five main steps: stock preparation and panel glue-up; making the front and rear leg assemblies; con-

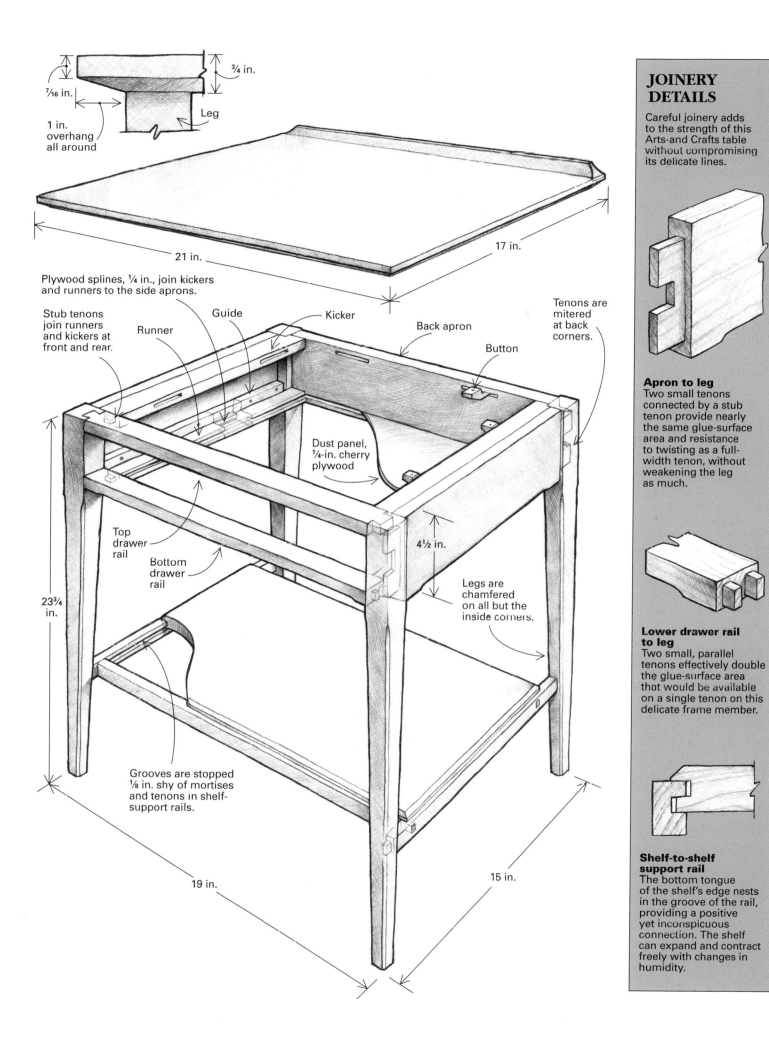

¾ in.

⁷⁄₁₆ in.

1 in.
overhang
all around

Leg

21 in.

17 in.

Plywood splines, ¼ in., join kickers
and runners to the side aprons.

Stub tenons
join runners
and kickers at
front and rear.

Runner

Guide

Kicker

Back apron

Button

Tenons are
mitered
at back
corners.

Dust panel,
¼-in. cherry
plywood

4½ in.

Top
drawer
rail

Bottom
drawer
rail

23¾
in.

Legs are
chamfered
on all but the
inside corners.

Grooves are stopped
⅛ in. shy of mortises
and tenons in shelf-
support rails.

19 in.

15 in.

JOINERY DETAILS

Careful joinery adds
to the strength of this
Arts-and-Crafts table
without compromising
its delicate lines.

Apron to leg
Two small tenons
connected by a stub
tenon provide nearly
the same glue-surface
area and resistance
to twisting as a full-
width tenon, without
weakening the leg
as much.

**Lower drawer rail
to leg**
Two small, parallel
tenons effectively double
the glue-surface area
that would be available
on a single tenon on this
delicate frame member.

**Shelf-to-shelf
support rail**
The bottom tongue
of the shelf's edge nests
in the groove of the rail,
providing a positive
yet inconspicuous
connection. The shelf
can expand and contract
freely with changes in
humidity.

Keeping track of the legs is easier when they're numbered on top, clockwise from the front left. This system helps prevent layout errors.

Marking out the dovetail socket—Scribing the socket from the bottom of the slightly tapered dovetail ensures a good fit in the leg.

necting these two assemblies (including making the shelf and its frame); making and fitting the drawer; and making and attaching the top.

Stock selection and preparation

I milled all the stock for this table to within 1/16 in. of final thickness and width. I also glued up the tabletop, the shelf and the drawer bottom right away to give them time to move a bit before planing them to final thickness. This helps ensure they'll stay flat in the finished piece. With these three panels in clamps, I dimensioned the rest of the parts to a hair over final thickness. I finish-planed them by hand just before marking out any joinery.

Making the front and rear assemblies

Layout began with the legs. I numbered them clockwise around the perimeter, beginning with the left front as I faced the piece, writing the numbers on the tops of the legs (see the top left photo). This system tells me where each leg goes, which

end of a leg is up and which face is which.

Dovetailing the top rail into the front legs— The dovetails that connect the top rail to the front legs taper slightly top to bottom. I used the narrower bottom of the dovetail to lay out the sockets in the legs. The slight taper ensures a snug fit (see the top right photo). Don't make the dovetails too large, or you'll weaken the legs.

After I marked, cut and chopped out the sockets, I tested the fit of these dovetails. By using clamping pads and hand screws across the joint, I eliminated the possibility of splitting the leg (see the photo at right). The dovetail should fit snugly but not tightly. Pare the socket, if necessary, until you have a good fit.

Tapering and mortising the legs— I tapered the two inside faces of each leg, beginning 4½ in. down from the top. I removed most of the waste on the jointer and finished the job with a handplane. The tapers must be flat. To avoid planing

Checking the fit of the top-rail dovetail—A hand screw prevents a leg from splitting if the dovetail is too big. The fit should be snug but not tight.

over a penciled reference line at the top of the taper, I drew hash marks across it. With each stroke of the plane, the lines got shorter. That let me know how close I was getting.

I cut the mortises for this table on a hollow-chisel mortiser. It's quick, and it keeps all the mortises consistent. I made sure all mortises that could be cut with

one setting were done at the same time, even if I didn't need the components right away.

Tenoning the aprons and drawer rail— I tenoned the sides, back and lower drawer rail on the tablesaw, using a double-blade tenoning setup (for more on that subject, see *FWW* #95, pp. 72-75). It takes a little time to get the cut right, but once a test piece fits, tenoning takes just a few minutes. After I cut the tenon cheeks on the tablesaw, I bandsawed just shy of the tenon shoulders and then pared to the line.

One wide apron tenon would have meant a very long mortise, weakening the leg. Instead, I divided the wide tenon into two small tenons separated by a stub tenon (see the drawing detail on p. 95). That left plenty of glue-surface area without a big hole in the leg.

Mortising for runners, kickers and buttons—The drawer rides on runners that are mortised into the lower front rail and the back apron. Similarly, the kickers at the tops of the side aprons, which prevent the drawer from drooping when open, are mortised into the top front rail and the back apron. I cut the ¼-in.-wide mortises for the runner and kicker tenons on the back edge of both drawer rails and on the back apron. There are eight mortises for the drawer runners and kickers. Another seven mortises of the same size are for the buttons that attach the top to the table's base—three on the back apron and two on each kicker.

I also cut grooves for the dust panel at this time. The ¼ in.-thick panel is set into the frame of the table just below the drawer. It's a nice touch, even if it's not needed structurally. I cut the grooves for the panel into the bottom of the back apron and into the back of the drawer rail. (I cut the dust-panel grooves in the drawer runners later.) Then I made a test-fit with a scrap of the same ¼-in. cherry plywood used for the panel.

Chamfering and gluing up—Stopped chamfers are routed on the legs and aprons of this table, each terminating in a carved lamb's tongue. I stopped routing just shy of the area to be carved and then carved the

tongue and the little shoulder in three steps, as shown in the photos at right.

Gluing up the table base is a two-step process. First I connected the front legs with the top and bottom drawer rails and the back legs with the back apron. To prevent the legs from toeing in or out because of clamping pressure, I inserted spacers between the legs at their feet and clamped both the top and bottom. Then I check for square, measuring diagonally from corner to corner (see the photo at left on p. 98). It ensures that the assembly is square and that the legs are properly spaced.

Connecting the front and rear assemblies

To hold the legs in position while I measured for the drawer runners and kickers and, later, to get the spacing on shelf-support rails correct, I made a simple frame of hardboard and wooden corner blocks (see the photo at right on p. 98). The frame ensures the assembly is square and the legs are properly spaced. After I marked the shoulder-to-shoulder lengths for the runners and kickers, I cut and fit the stub tenons that join these pieces to the front and rear assemblies. The back ends of the runners and kickers must be notched to fit around the inside corners of the legs.

Runners, kickers and dust panel—I cut the ¼-in. grooves for the dust panel in the drawer runners next. I also cut grooves for the splines with which I connected the drawer runners and kickers to the sides of the table. There are 10 grooves in all—one each on the inside and outside edges of the drawer runners, one on the outside edge of each of the kickers and two in each side for the splines.

Then I dry-clamped the table and made sure the tops of the kickers were flush with the top edges of the sides, the tops of

the runners flush with the top of the drawer rail and the bottoms of the runners flush with the bottom edges of the sides. Then I cut the dust panel to size, test-fit it and set it aside until glue-up.

Building the shelf frame and shelf—The shelf on this table is a floating panel captured by a frame made of four rails. The two rails that run front to back are tenoned into the legs; the other two are joined to the first pair with through-wedged tenons.

I put the dry-assembled table into the hardboard frame and clamped the legs to the blocks. Then I clamped the pair of rails that will be tenoned into the legs against the inside surfaces of the legs and marked the shoulder of each tenon (see the photo at right on p. 98). I also marked the rails for orientation so that the shoulders can be mated correctly with the legs.

Tenons were cut and fit next. With the rails dry-clamped into the legs, I measured for the two remaining rails to be joined to the first pair. I laid out and cut the through-mortises in the first set of rails, chopping halfway in from each side to prevent tearout. I cut the tenons on the second set of rails, assembled the frame and marked the through-tenons with a pencil line for wedge orientation. So they don't split the rails, the wedges must be perpendicular to the grain of the mortised rail.

I flared the sides of the through-mortises (not the tops and bottoms) so the outside of the mortise is about ¹⁄₁₆ in. wider than the inside. This taper, which goes about three-quarters of the way into the mortise, lets the wedges splay the tenon, locking the rail into the mortise like a dovetail.

Next I marked the location of the wedge kerfs in each tenon, scribing a line from both sides of the tenon with a marking gauge for uniformity. I cut the

Step 1: Pare to marked baseline. *Strive for a fair, even curve, and cut down toward the chamfer.*

Step 2: Tap a stop for the shoulder at the baseline. *Avoid cutting too deeply; just a light tap is needed.*

Step 3: Pare into stop to create a shoulder. *You have to cut toward the shoulder, so take light cuts and watch which way the grain is running. If you must pare against the grain, make sure your chisel is freshly honed.*

Check diagonals to make sure assemblies are glued up square. Clamps and a spacer at the bottom of the legs prevent the clamping pressure at the top from causing the legs to toe in or out.

Simple frame keeps legs spaced accurately and the base of the table square. A ¼-in.-thick piece of hardboard and some scrap blocks make up this handy frame. With the legs properly spaced, the author can mark the shoulders of the shelf-frame rail against the tapered legs as well as take precise measurements for runner and kicker lengths.

kerfs at a slight angle. Wedges must fill both the kerf and the gap in the widened mortise, so they need to be just over ¹⁄₁₆ in. thick at their widest.

An interlocking tongue and groove connects the shelf to the rails that support it (see the drawing detail on p. 95). Using a ¼-in. slot cutter in my table-mounted router, I cut the groove in the rails, working out the fit on test pieces first. The slots are ¼ in. deep. I stopped the grooves in the rails ¹⁄₈ in. or so short of the mortises on the side rails and short of the tenon shoulders on the front and back

rails. I notched the shelf to fit at the corners (see the drawing).

I measured the space between the rails of the shelf frame and added ½ in. in each direction to get the shelf dimensions. I cut the tongue on all four edges on the router table.

Gluing up the shelf-frame assembly— Before gluing up the shelf frame, I routed hollows in clamp pads to fit over the through-tenons on two of the shelf rails. Then I began gluing up the shelf assembly. I applied glue sparingly in the mortises and on the tenons so I

wouldn't accidentally glue the shelf in place. I pulled the joints tight with clamps and then removed the clamps temporarily so I could insert the wedges.

After tapping the lightly glue-coated wedges into the kerfs in the tenons, I reclamped the frame. I checked diagonals and adjusted the clamps until the assembly was square. Once the glue was dry, I sawed off the protruding tenons and wedges and planed them flush.

Overall glue-up— With the shelf frame glued up, the entire table was ready to be assem-

bled. I began the large front-to-back glue-up by dry-clamping the front and back leg assemblies, sides, runners, kickers (with splines), dust panel and shelf assembly. I made adjustments and then glued up.

I made and fit the drawer guides next (see the drawing for placement). I glued the guides to both the sides and the runners and screwed them to the sides with deeply counter-sunk brass screws.

I did a thorough cleanup of the table in preparation for drawer fitting. I removed remaining glue, ironed out dents

and sanded the entire piece with 120-grit sandpaper on a block. I gently pared sharp corners, taking care not to lose overall crispness.

The drawer

I particularly enjoy making and fitting drawers. A well-made drawer that whispers in and out gives me great satisfaction. I use the traditional British system of drawermaking, which produces what my teachers called a piston fit. The process is painstaking (see *FWW* #73, pp. 48-51 for a description of this method), but the results are well-worth

the effort. That, however, is a story for another day.

Making and attaching the top

After I thicknessed and cut the top to size, I placed it face down on my bench. I set the glued-up base upside down on the top and oriented it so it would have a 1-in. overhang all around. I marked the positions of the outside corners and connected them with a pencil line around the perimeter. This line is one edge of the bevel on the underside of the top. Then I used a marking gauge to strike

a line 7/16 in. from the top surface on all four edges. Connecting the two lines at the edges created the bevel angle (see the drawing on p. 95). I roughed out the bevel on the tablesaw and cleaned it up with a plane. The bevels should appear to grow out of the tops of the legs.

Making and attaching the coved lip—The cove at the back of the top is a strip set into a rabbet at the back. I cut the cove from the same board I used for the top so that grain and color would match closely. I ripped the cove strip on the tablesaw and handplaned it to fit the rabbet. I shaped the strip on the router table, leaving the point at which it intersects the top slightly proud. To provide even clamping pressure, I used a rabbeted caul, clamping both down and in (see the photo at right above).

When the glue was dry, I planed the back and the ends of the cove flush with the top. To form a smooth transition between top and cove in front, I used a curved scraper, followed by sandpaper on a block shaped to fit the cove. I frequently checked the transition with my hand and sanded a wider swath toward the end. It's easy to go too far and have a nasty dip in front of the cove.

I drew the ends of the cove

with a French curve and then shaped the ends with a coping saw, chisel and sandpaper. The curve should blend into the tabletop seamlessly.

Finishing up with oil—After finish-sanding, I applied several coats of raw linseed oil diluted with mineral spirits in a 50/50 mix, a few more coats of straight linseed oil and, finally, two to three coats of tung oil to harden the surface. I let the oil dry thoroughly between coats. After the last coat of oil was dry, I rubbed the surface down with a Scotch-Brite pad and gave the table a few coats of paste wax. The drawer was the exception: Aside from the face of the drawer front, all other surfaces were finished with wax alone.

Attaching the top—I screwed the top to the top-drawer rail from beneath to fix its position at the front. That way, the mating of the bevel with the front rail will be correct and any seasonal movement of the top will be at the back. I attached the top to the base with buttons on the sides and in the rear.   □

Stephen Lamont is a professional furnituremaker. He recently accepted a position as craftsman with the Edward Barnsley Educational Trust in Hampshire, England.

Fig. 1: Cabriole leg pattern

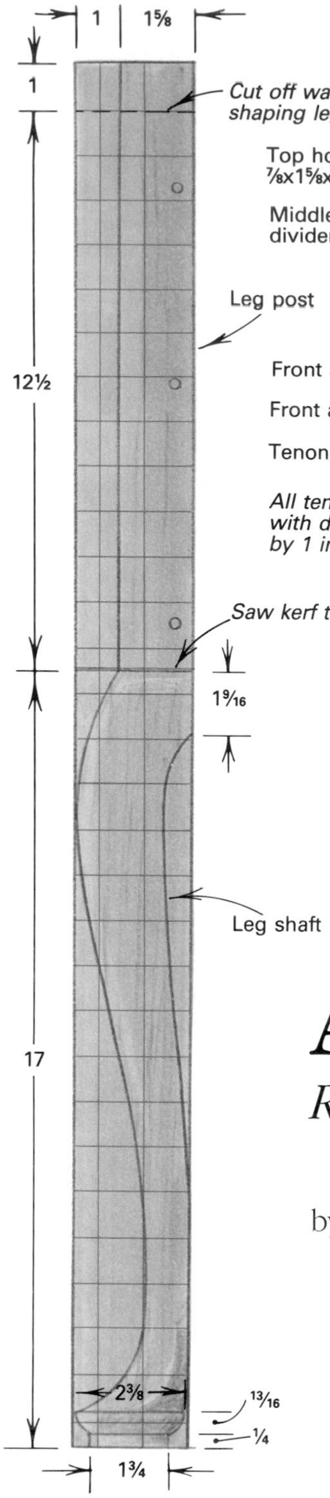

1
1 5/8
1
Cut off waste after shaping leg.
12½
Leg post
Saw kerf to define knee.
1 9/16
17
Leg shaft
2⅜
13/16
¼
1¾

Fig. 2: Connecticut Lowboy

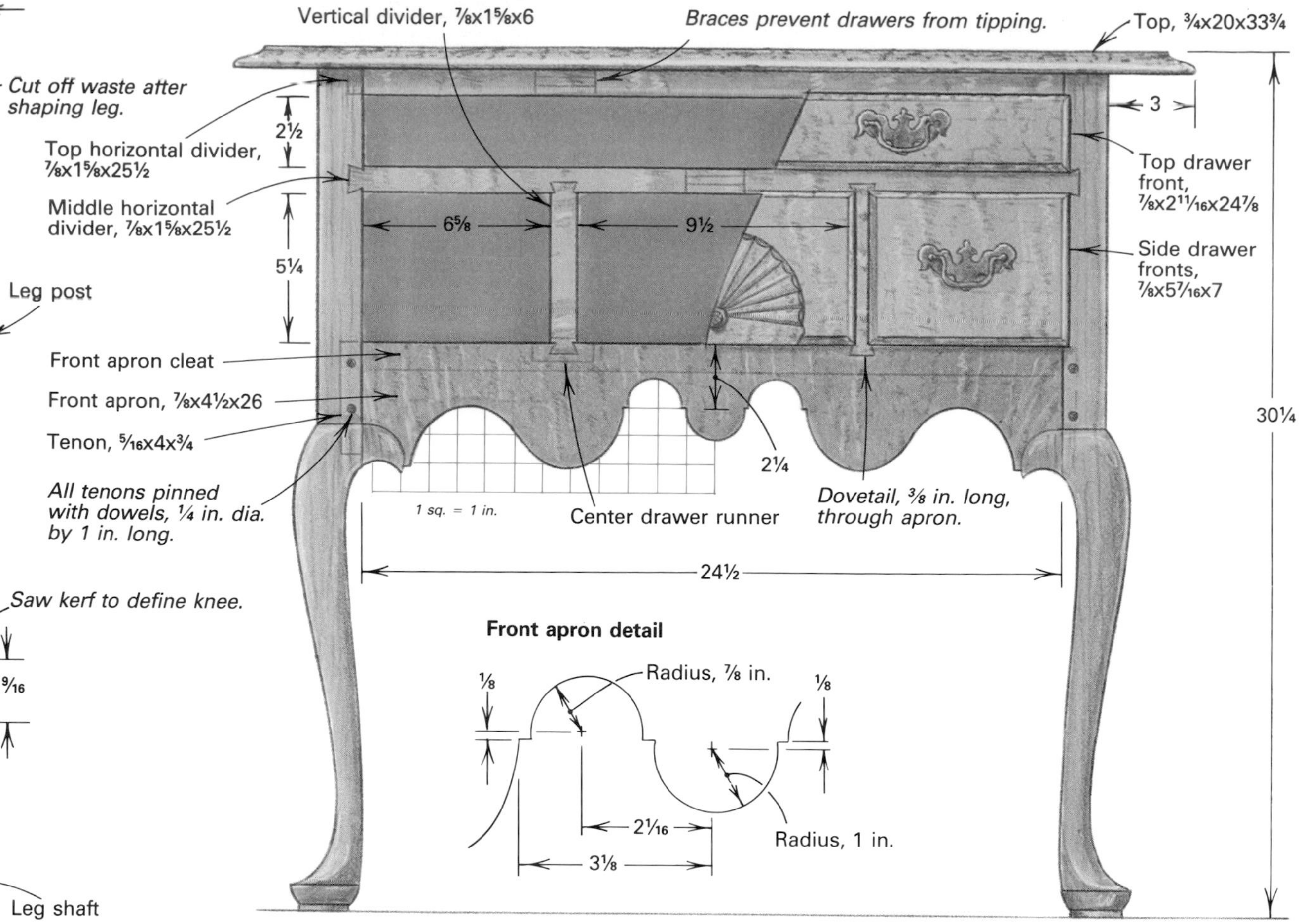

Vertical divider, 7/8x1 5/8x6
Braces prevent drawers from tipping.
Top, 3/4x20x33 3/4
3
Top drawer front, 7/8x2 11/16x24 7/8
Side drawer fronts, 7/8x5 7/16x7
30¼
Top horizontal divider, 7/8x1 5/8x25½
2½
Middle horizontal divider, 7/8x1 5/8x25½
5¼
6⅝
9½
Front apron cleat
Front apron, 7/8x4½x26
Tenon, 5/16x4x3/4
All tenons pinned with dowels, ¼ in. dia. by 1 in. long.
2¼
1 sq. = 1 in.
Center drawer runner
Dovetail, 3/8 in. long, through apron.
24½
Front apron detail
⅛
Radius, 7/8 in.
⅛
2 1/16
3⅛
Radius, 1 in.

A Queen Anne Dressing Table

Reproducing an 18th-century lowboy

by Norm Vandal

The Queen Anne dressing table is a rather special woodworking project. The piece itself is beautiful, a lovely example of the fine lines and proportions that characterized the period. And it is a perfect exercise in all aspects of 18th-century cabinetmaking skills, including mortise-and-tenon carcase construction, sculptured cabriole legs with turned-pad feet, shell carving and drawer dovetailing. When you've completed a dressing table, you've really made a table *and* a small chest of drawers, so you will have mastered many of the skills needed to produce other period pieces.

Queen Anne dressing tables actually date back to the first half of the 18th century. They were extremely popular during this period because they are attractive and multifunctional, capable of serving not only as a dressing table, but also as a side or serving table and a basic work surface. Most people today call this furniture form a lowboy, although that term didn't appear until the end of the 19th century, when it was mentioned in the August, 1899, issue of *House Beautiful*. Frequently made as companions to matching high chests, called highboys, Queen Anne dressing tables were scaled-down versions of the base on highboys, with all the same features and basic proportions, hence the term lowboy.

The delicate and graceful nature of the lowboy's form suggests it is a feminine piece. Designed to be placed against a wall, its top is seldom molded on the back edge, as it invariably is at the front and sides. Additionally, the backboard is usually made of a secondary wood, such as pine or chestnut, and is obviously intended to be hidden. The lowboy I've designed adheres closely to the essential elements of the Queen Anne period. So while the result isn't an authentic reproduction, it could well have been an

Drawings: Lee Hov

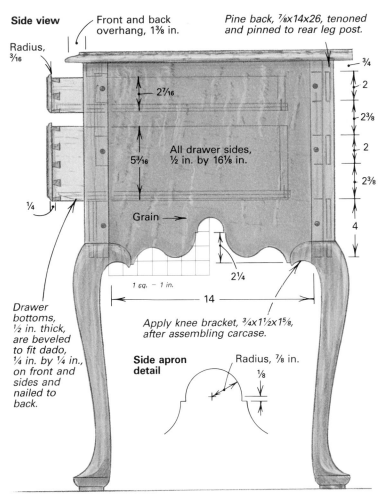

Side view

Front and back overhang, 1³⁄₈ in.

Radius, ³⁄₁₆

Pine back, ⁷⁄₈x14x26, tenoned and pinned to rear leg post.

¾

2

2⁷⁄₁₆

2³⁄₈

5⁹⁄₁₆   All drawer sides, ½ in. by 16¹⁄₈ in.

2

¼

2³⁄₈

Grain →

4

1 sq. − 1 in.

2¼

14

Drawer bottoms, ½ in. thick, are beveled to fit dado, ¼ in. by ¼ in., on front and sides and nailed to back.

Apply knee bracket, ¾x1½x1⁵⁄₈, after assembling carcase.

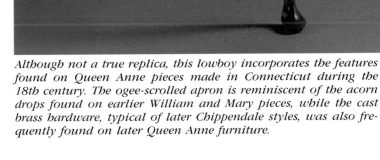

Side apron detail

Radius, ⁷⁄₈ in.

⅛

Although not a true replica, this lowboy incorporates the features found on Queen Anne pieces made in Connecticut during the 18th century. The ogee-scrolled apron is reminiscent of the acorn drops found on earlier William and Mary pieces, while the cast brass hardware, typical of later Chippendale styles, was also frequently found on later Queen Anne furniture.

18th-century New England piece. The lines of my dressing table are quite similar to pieces typically made in Connecticut, although cherry would probably have been the preferred wood instead of the tiger maple I used. Acorn drops, vestiges of the William and Mary period, have been omitted and the apron has a deep, ogee-scrolled profile. The top drawer also reflects the period preference over earlier three-drawer arrangements. The fan carving, sometimes referred to as a sunburst, is really a stylized shell, another trademark of Queen Anne furniture.

Making the cabriole legs—The cabriole legs, which extend the full height of the dressing table, greatly enhance the structural integrity of Queen Anne pieces, but they have one serious drawback: the grain on the leg posts runs in opposite directions to that on the case sides. Seasonal expansion and contraction of the case sides resulted in cracks on many Queen Anne and Chippendale highboys and lowboys. However, to maintain the authenticity of the piece, I have joined the case frame in the traditional manner.

Proceed by milling the leg blank square, making it large enough to accommodate the offset leg post and the curve of the leg shaft, shown in figures 1 and 2 on the facing page. Cut the blank clean and square at both ends, leaving an extra inch on the leg post end. This keeps the lathe drive center from damaging the finished leg post and prevents scrapers, planes and sanding blocks from diving off the end of the stock, thereby altering the shape of the post. Any imperfections are easily removed by cutting off the extra inch after the leg is completed.

Begin laying out the legs by making a full-size template for the legs based on the dimensions given in figures 1 and 2. Then, draw layout lines in pencil across the blank to mark the leg's main transitions: the top of the foot, the top of the knee (the bottom of the

leg post), the length of the shoulder where the knee bracket will attach and the exact finished length of the leg, plus the extra inch at the top of the post. Clamping the four leg blanks together will speed up the layout and ensure that all the legs will be identical. Use a marking gauge to lay out the width of the leg posts. The incised gauge lines are more accurate and easier to follow than pencil lines, which are easily smudged and too thick for precision.

Trace the curve of the leg on the blanks while holding the template so the back of the leg post and the back of the foot are flush with one edge of the blank. Reposition the template on the adjoining face, aligning the back of the template with the same corner, and trace again. The intersecting corner forms the inside of the leg, so orient the pattern to present the best figure on the leg's front.

For the turned-pad foot, draw diagonals from corner to corner on both ends of the blank and mark the center with an awl or punch. Consult the leg detail in figure 1, and then use a pencil compass to draw the major diameter of the foot, 2⅜ in., and the smaller pad, 1¾ in., on the bottom of the blank. Make the lines dark, so they can be seen while the stock is rotating on the lathe. This will enable you to turn the feet to the correct diameters without using calipers.

Before mounting the blank on the lathe make a single crosscut, as shown in the detail in figure 1, into each of the two adjacent outside faces of the blank to separate the top of the knee from the post, which is not cut to size until after the leg is carved. The crosscut makes a clear stopping point for carving the cabriole leg and the oversized post will be easier to clamp in the vise and turn on the lathe. The full-dimension blank will not only be better balanced on the lathe, but it will prevent the drive center from being dangerously close to the edges, as it is with a fully sawn post. Also, the leg post is less likely to become marred during carving. Now, following the template pattern you traced earlier, bandsaw the leg shape out of the square blank. Cut the inside and outside contours on one face first, save the waste and then tape it back on the blank to bandsaw the other face.

Study the detail of the leg given in figure 1 for the general shape and dimensions to complete the legs. To begin, center the bandsawn leg on the lathe, with the foot at the tailstock end, and turn the major diameter of the foot. Next, mark the height of the foot pad on the cylinder, and then turn the pad to size, shaping the sides of the foot to the correct profile. I scrape the pad with a parting tool because it's difficult to cut with a gouge or skew in such a small area. Use the tip of a skew chisel to make a shallow groove at the top of the foot as a reference point for carving the foot and the ankle. You can also turn a small shoulder above the incised line, which rounds off the arris at the back of the ankle and causes the three other thin corners to flake off. With the skew, shape the curved profile of the foot and turn a crisp corner between the upper part of the foot and the pad. Then, sand the foot on the lathe.

Shape the lower leg, from the knee to the top of the foot, using a drawknife, followed by a spokeshave, a patternmaker's rasp and cabinet scrapers. This may be done right on the lathe or by clamping the leg in a vise. Pare the back of the ankle a bit beyond the bandsawn line for a more graceful definition. I bandsaw the leg post, keeping the sawn face as smooth as possible, and then use a scraper to smooth its surface. A knife cut at the top of the knee helps maintain crisp definition between the knee and the post. With a chisel, pare the sawmarks off the knee and smooth it with a patternmaker's rasp and a file, but leave the shoulder crisp where the knee bracket will be applied. Finish up smoothing and shaping the leg by sanding. The inside curve of the leg, underneath and behind the bracket, is simply pared with a chisel and carving gouges, and need not be sanded.

Case and drawer construction—Although sugar, or hard, maple is the most common native hardwood used in Queen Anne furniture, most Connecticut lowboys were made from cherry, a wood that was favored either because of its availability or because it is easily finished to resemble the more stylish imported mahogany. I chose tiger maple as the primary wood for this piece because of its incredible beauty, in spite of the difficulty of carving the fan in

The central drawer runners are mortised into the back of the carcase and rest on a cleat nailed to the back of the front apron. A brace mortised into the back of the carcase and into the middle horizontal divider keeps this drawer from tipping when opened.

such wild grain. For the sides and top I was fortunate to have available full-width tiger-maple stock. The back was made from a single, wide pine board and all internal drawer parts, as well as the cleats and drawer runners, were also made from pine.

I made the sides and the back out of one-piece, 14-in.-wide boards; if you need to glue up the sides, do not use more than two boards for authenticity. Cut tenons on the sides and back, as shown in figure 2 on pp. 100-101 and figure 3 on the facing page, and chop their respective mortises in the legs. The mortises are located so the outside of the leg posts will be flush with the sides and back. Make a cardboard template (I prefer oak tag) from the dimensions in figure 2, and then clamp the side pieces together to bandsaw the scallops on the bottom of both sides. After test-fitting the joints, you can begin work on the front of the case.

The front apron is tenoned into the leg posts in the same way as the side and back panels. Prepare the apron stock as shown in figure 1 on p. 100, and cut the tenons on both ends. Then, use a cardboard template to lay out the scalloped profile and bandsaw it as you did the side panels. After making the front apron, joint and plane the two horizontal dividers and cut the dovetails on both ends. The shoulder-to-shoulder length of the horizontal dividers is identical to the shoulder-to-shoulder length of the front apron. The top divider is dovetailed into the endgrain at the top of the leg posts, which holds the case together. I've seen rectangular tenons used to install this member, but dovetails are probably stronger here and were more common. (For more information on cutting sliding dovetails, see *FWW* #79, pp. 54-57.) Scribe the dovetail pockets from the horizontal dividers themselves and cut them into the front leg posts. As you proceed, check the joints for accuracy so they will fit perfectly. Lay out and cut the pockets for the vertical dividers on the top of the apron and the underside of the lower horizontal divider.

I usually wait until after the piece is assembled to cut the two short, vertical dividers to length. This way I can measure the required length directly from the piece and have more room to install the central drawer runners and the front apron cleat that supports them. The two central runners for the three bottom drawers are mortised into the backboard, as shown in the photo below, and sit on a cleat nailed to the inside of the front apron, as shown in figure 3 on the facing page. Pockets in the cleat keep the runners in position. The outside runners are nailed directly to the case sides. In addition, two braces mortised into the top horizontal divider and the backboard, and another brace mortised into the middle divider and the backboard, shown in the photo at left, prevent the top and center drawers from tipping when pulled out. The outside runners for the top drawer prevent the two outside bottom drawers from tipping. Lay out and cut all of the mortises for these braces and runners in the horizontal dividers, the backboard and the apron cleat. Then, dimension the three braces and cut the tenons.

Now you can begin to assemble the case. I like to start by gluing the two back legs to the backboard, and the front apron and horizontal dividers to the front legs. Make sure that the front section is square; the back should be squared automatically by the shoulders on the wide backboards. The back and front assemblies will sandwich the rest of the case. With the back placed flat on the workbench, test-fit the sides in the rear legs and insert the three braces into the mortises in the backboard. Then add the glued-up front assembly to complete the sandwich. If everything fits well, disassemble the case and put it together again with all joints glued and clamped. After the glue has set, pin the tenons for the sides, back and front apron in the leg posts.

Rabbet a piece of 1⅛-in.-square pine to form the four L-shape drawer runners that are nailed directly onto the case sides, as

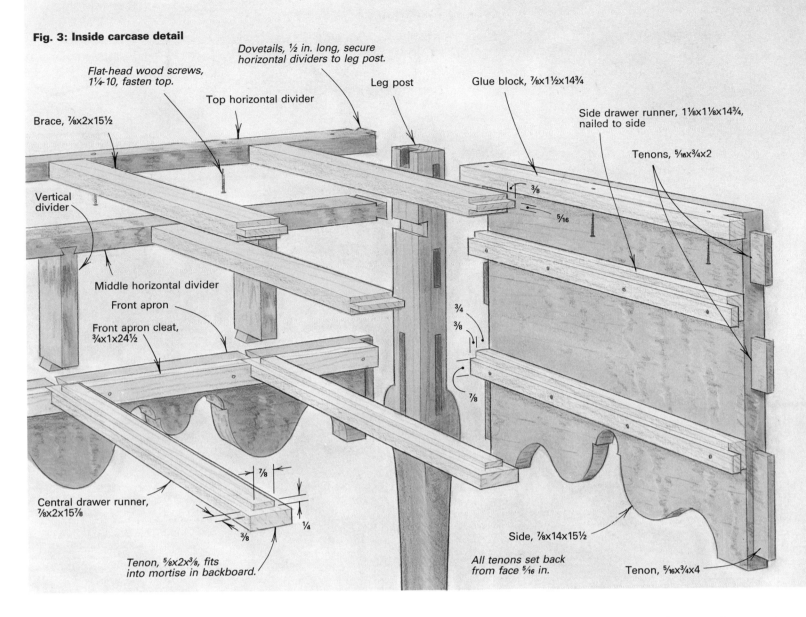

Fig. 3: Inside carcase detail

Flat-head wood screws, 1¼-10, fasten top.

Dovetails, ½ in. long, secure horizontal dividers to leg post.

Top horizontal divider

Leg post

Glue block, ⅞x1½x14¾

Side drawer runner, 1⅛x1⅛x14¾, nailed to side

Brace, ⅞x2x15½

Tenons, ⁵⁄₁₆x¾x2

Vertical divider

⅜

⁵⁄₁₆

Middle horizontal divider

Front apron

¾

⅜

Front apron cleat, ¾x1x24½

⅞

⅞

¼

⅜

Central drawer runner, ⅞x2x15⅞

Tenon, ⅝x2x⅜, fits into mortise in backboard.

Side, ⅞x14x15½

All tenons set back from face ⁵⁄₁₆ in.

Tenon, ⁵⁄₁₆x¾x4

shown in figure 3. These runners support the top drawer and one side of both outside bottom drawers. Make the two T-shape central runners that serve all three bottom drawers as detailed in figure 3. They are glued and slipped in place once the cleat has been nailed to the front apron, and their rear tenons are fitted to their respective mortises in the backboard. Now cut the two vertical dividers to length, dovetail both ends and glue them in place.

The drawer construction for this lowboy is typical of the period, as shown in figure 2 on pp. 100-101. Its sides and the top of all drawer fronts are rabbeted to overlap the front of the case, and all the edges are lip-molded the same as the shell front drawer shown in figure 4 on p. 105. While the drawer sides join the back with through dovetails, the front is joined with half-blind dovetails. The underside of the ½-in.-thick bottom is beveled along the front and sides, like a raised panel, to fit into a ¼-in. dado in the front and sides. The bottom slides under the drawer back and is nailed to the back's bottom edge. I size the drawers to allow ¹⁄₁₆-in. clearance between the drawer and the opening on the top and each side.

Do not assemble the central bottom drawer until after the shell carving is finished. You can prepare all the rabbets, the lip molding and the dovetailing, but the unattached drawer front is much easier to carve.

Applied knee brackets—The knee bracket serves to balance the protruding knee of a sculptured cabriole leg and visually separates

the leg from the apron, easing the transition between the curved knee and the flat apron. It also reinforces whatever scroll work or scalloped carving is employed in the design of the apron. An applied bracket, as used on this lowboy, is glued to the corner formed by the protruding leg shoulder and the face of the apron. As shown in figures 1 and 2, the bracket usually terminates in a point or a scrolled bead, pointing down and away from the apron. Sometimes an applied bracket runs the full length of the apron, between the knees of the legs at both ends. However, this type of bracket is commonly found on tea tables or sometimes on the ends of a lowboy or highboy base, and the bottom edge of this full-apron knee bracket is generally scrolled.

The size and proportion of the knee bracket are important to the overall design of a piece of furniture, so make the drawings and templates for the bracket as you develop the rest of the design. Begin making the knee brackets after the legs have been fully shaped, sanded and attached to the apron. Some people prefer to apply the bracket to the leg and carve it before the leg is joined to the rest of the piece. Although the individual legs are easier to hold on the bench, I prefer to fit the bracket to the leg and the apron after the two adjacent surfaces have been permanently joined.

I make all the knee brackets for a piece of furniture out of one piece of wood. This large stock is easy to grasp when bandsawing the bracket profiles, and it enables me to keep my fingers away from the blade. The thickness of the bracket stock is easily determined by measuring the distance that the knee protrudes beyond

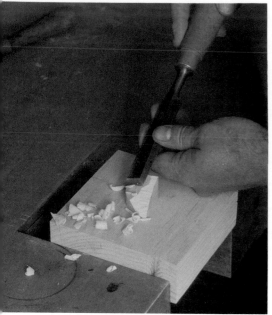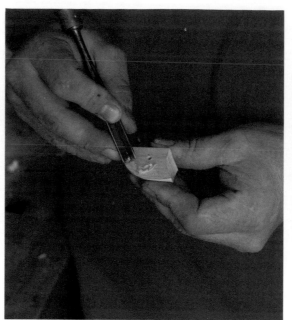

The knee bracket is firmly held for carving by a drywall screw through a scrap block that is clamped in a bench vise (left). A small groove carved on the back of the knee bracket (center) traps excess glue and prevents squeeze-out on the face of the apron dur- *ing glue-up. The tool marks from the gouge even up the underside of the joint between the knee bracket and the leg and further add to the authenticity of this piece (right). The face of this joint is smoothed with files and sandpaper to match the contour of the leg.*

the face of the apron. I usually add another ¹⁄₁₆ in. to ⅛ in. to this measurement to account for any variation between the other knees on the piece. The width of the bracket stock is determined by the width of the brackets, as indicated in figure 2. Make the stock at least 4 in. or 5 in. longer than the total height of all your brackets to provide a handle when you saw the last bracket. Try to match the bracket stock to the legs in both color and grain pattern and run the grain in the bracket in the same vertical direction as the grain in the leg. You may need to go through a bunch of stock to find a piece that will match a highly figured wood like tiger maple, but then again, knee brackets don't amount to very much material.

To determine the shape of the knee bracket, hold the stock against the apron and the vertical leg shoulder and trace the contour of the knee. Trace all the brackets against their respective knees, and number the brackets and leg shoulders accordingly. Make a template from your front-view drawing and use it to transfer the outline to the bracket. Then, bandsaw the bracket from the stock and use a chisel to shape the curve on the outside of the bracket. A thin drywall screw holds the tiny knee bracket to a small carving platform, which is clamped in a vise, as shown in the left photo above. Smooth the curve with a file and finish the bracket with sandpaper.

Before gluing the bracket in place, cut a shallow groove on its back, about ⅛ in. from the top edge, as shown in the center photo above. This groove will trap any excess glue and eliminate squeeze-out onto the apron when the bracket is applied. Spread glue on the surface behind the groove and on the other vertical face, which attaches to the leg. Do not apply glue to the apron or leg. Then, press the glued-on bracket in position for a couple of minutes, until it doesn't fall off. If you've made a tight-fitting shoulder, the bracket should stay without any fastenings or clamping. When the glue has set, use a chisel to pare the joint between the bracket and the leg, and sand it smooth. A gouge can be used to smooth the concave area of the joint on the underside of the bracket, as shown in the right photo above. Textures are important in period furniture reproductions, so you needn't make this surface machine perfect.

Carving the shell—One of the most important characteristics of Queen Anne case furniture is the judicious use of carved motifs. Shells, or shell-like fans or sunbursts were most popular and often carved on the drawer fronts of highboys and lowboys. No better decorative element could have been drawn from nature to lend emphasis to the graceful lines of Queen Anne furniture.

The surface of the hub is flush with the face of the drawer front, while the recessed area below the hub is carved to the depth of the front apron. The quickest and most accurate way to determine the depth of this recess is to set the drawer face in its opening and scribe a line on the bottom edge of the drawer front along the face of the apron.

Laying out the fan on the drawer front is done in stages as the carving progresses. Begin by locating the center point, from which the fan's radii are drawn, on the vertical centerline of the drawer front, ¹¹⁄₁₆ in. above the bottom edge. Using a small divider with a sharpened leg, scribe the 1-in.-dia. center hub. The scribed line will help guide the carving chisels. Scribe the fan's 6½-in. diameter onto the drawer face, and then scribe a 6⅛-in.-dia. circle inside the larger one to represent the width of the arc termini of the rays. The rays terminate in arc segments of ¾-in.-dia. circles and are ⅝ in. wide where they contact the circumference of the fan. Because the fan's center point is located above the bottom edge of the drawer, the fan covers more than 180°, as shown in figure 4 on the facing page, but it terminates at the edge of the lip molding.

There are 17 rays, and the odd one is centered on the vertical centerline of the drawer front. After you have located the central ray, set your dividers to ⅝ in. and lay out the other rays. Use a ¾-in.-dia. round template made of lightweight metal, such as aluminum flashing, to lay out the arcs of the ray termini. Notice that the rays are S-shape in cross section to mimic the undulating contour of concave shell carvings. Carving the rays is simplified if the entire ray area is first relief-carved to a uniform contour, as shown in figure 4. Shape this area with shallow-radius gouges, and smooth it with coarse sandpaper.

Each ray must now be defined on the contoured field. Simply draw the rays on the surface using a pencil and a flexible straight-edge as a guide. The rays are spaced a bit less than ⅛ in. apart at the hub, and this can be determined by eye or laid out with dividers.

Fan carvings do not require a huge assortment of carving chisels; gouges can be used to shape convex surfaces as well as concave surfaces. To begin carving the rays, first incise a shallow groove along the layout lines using a straight chisel. Then, use a V-parting tool to begin to define the rays. The V-parting tool is useful only during the early stages of the carving. I use a combination of straight chisels and gouges to create the convex lobes, although any tool that works well for you is appropriate.

Lightly define the arc termini with a gouge of the correct sweep or incise them carefully with an X-Acto knife. Do not cut too deeply, but just enough to define a crisp edge. The convex lobes must be carved so that they end neatly at these termini, and various chisels and gouges will get the job done.

When all the rays are fully carved, sand them lightly with tiny pieces of folded, 120-grit paper. Shell carvings need not be sanded perfectly smooth, and, in fact, a few carved facets will add to the semblance of authenticity. I try to make my carvings as smooth as possible using chisels and gouges; I sand very little because it quickly dulls a crisp edge and diminishes the lively character of a carving. Burnishing can be effective, especially in the grooves of this fan carving. Rub these areas with a flat stick of hardwood sharpened to a knife edge, and renew the edge as it becomes dull from abrasion.

Finally, use a sharp knife to incise the circumference of the fan and carve the arc termini to meet it. The layout line will enable you to remove the chips cleanly. When the carving is complete, finish assembling the drawer and test it for fit. (Mack Headley offers more on carving a scallop shell in *FWW* #61, pp. 47-51.)

Installing the top—This lowboy has a top that is made from one 20-in.-wide board of exquisite tiger maple. This is an exceptionally large dimension for any native hardwood, so two boards are usually glued together. Again, three boards are almost never seen on period pieces and should be avoided on a reproduction.

The ogee-shape edge of the top can be cut with a router or roughed-out on a tablesaw and carved by hand. Because the shape does not conform to any standard router bit, a little experimentation will be necessary if you decide to use that method. You could also make several passes at various depths and distances from the edge with a ½-in. core-box router bit to shape the concave portion. The rest of the contour can be shaped with a block plane and scraped and sanded smooth by hand. The top is fastened to the base with 10, 10-1¼ flat-head wood screws, which are driven through the top horizontal divider and the glue blocks that are attached to the case sides, as shown in figure 3 on p. 103.

Finishing—The choice of finishing materials and application methods will determine, more than anything else, how a piece will look. The techniques I offer reflect my own attitudes toward making Queen Anne furniture and represent the fruit of many trials and errors. I strongly suggest that you experiment with whatever finish you plan to use before applying it to a piece of furniture, and keep a written journal of these experiments and their results.

I find it easiest to handplane, scrape or sand the furniture components before they are assembled. Period furnituremakers probably did the same, particularly since sandpaper was a precious commodity. They expended little energy in smoothing tool marks or surface imperfections where they wouldn't show, as on the underside of a tabletop or the inside of a chest of drawers.

To me, wood coloration is a two step process. The first step produces a base color, which homogenizes the various parts of a piece into a unified whole and serves as a foundation for stains

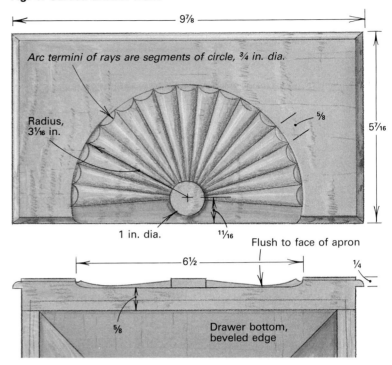

Fig. 4: Carved drawer front

Arc termini of rays are segments of circle, ¾ in. dia.

Radius, 3¹⁄₁₆ in.

⁵⁄₈

5⁷⁄₁₆

9⁷⁄₈

1 in. dia.

¹¹⁄₁₆

Flush to face of apron

6½

¼

⁵⁄₈

Drawer bottom, beveled edge

and paints applied in the second step. Aniline dyes produce a good base color: they penetrate well, without masking the wood's natural figure. Although it is particularly difficult to color maple so that it looks antique, I've had good success by first applying Lockwood's Early American Maple (available from W.D. Lockwood and Co. Inc., 83 Franklin St., New York, N.Y. 10013), an amber aniline dye, as a base color.

After the dye is fully dry, lightly sand the raised grain with 220-grit (or finer) paper. You will have to reburnish the fan carving and maybe touch up the lobes with 400-grit sandpaper. Then coat the piece with graining liquid (available from Stulb, Box 297, Norristown, Pa. 19404) and rub it off immediately, leaving residue in cracks and corners to tone down the aniline dye and add some artificial aging to the piece.

For a top coat, I want an easy-to-repair hard surface film that can be built up with three or four coats. I used to mix my own oil-and-varnish solutions, but I've found Minwax Antique Oil Finish (available from The Woodworkers' Store, 21801 Industrial Blvd., Rogers, Minn. 55374-9514), a mixture of linseed oil, varnish, tung oil and mineral spirits, to be effective right from the can. Applied with a brush or rag, it becomes tacky in a few minutes and can be buffed to a glossy sheen. At least three coats are required to produce a good finish. The only drawback of this product is its short shelf life, so buy it fresh and in small quantities. Drawer sides, backs and bottoms are sealed with a single coat of a mixture of two parts boiled linseed oil and one part turpentine.

Hardware—Casting was the most practical method of producing back plates and escutcheons and it is still the preferred method for the best and most historically accurate hardware. I use authentic cast hardware from Ball and Ball, 463 W. Lincoln Highway, Exton, Pa. 19341: four brass pulls (#C9-036 antique), one brass escutcheon (#C9-036E antique) and one ⁵⁄₈-in.-dia. brass knob (#G17-136 antique). □

Norm Vandal is a Consulting Editor for FWW *and a professional woodworker from Roxbury, Vt. He wrote a book on Queen Anne furniture, published by The Taunton Press in 1990.*

An Inconspicuous Vanity Table

Hinged lid reveals makeup and mirror

by Terry Moore

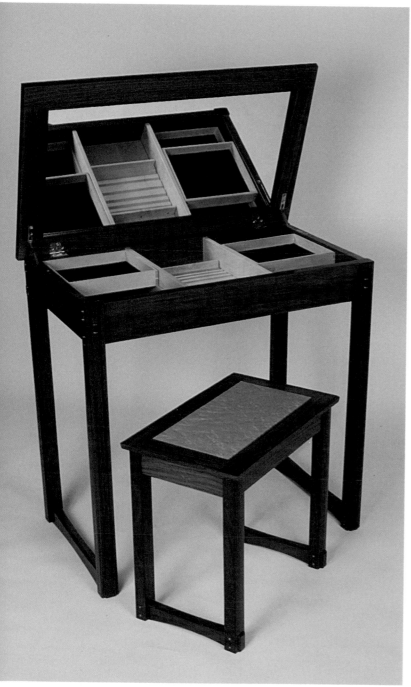

The author's oriental-style vanity table and matching stool are of contrasting East Indian rosewood and bird's-eye maple. Moore used maple wedges to secure the aprons' protruding through tenons to the legs. Removable velvet-lined jewelry and makeup trays are hidden under the vanity's mirrored lid.

I got the idea for this vanity while watching my wife put on her makeup in the bathroom, walk to her jewelry box in the bedroom, and then walk to a mirror on the other side of the room to put on earrings. The whole process seemed unnecessarily convoluted to me and I thought that if this ritual could be simplified, it would be more enjoyable. My vanity stores both jewelry and makeup and has a mirror conveniently located inside its hinged lid, which hides everything when closed.

The vanity's design is based on 18th- and 19th-century Korean furniture, and its frame-and-panel lid, as well as the stool seat, are highlighted with spectacularly contrasting East Indian rosewood and bird's-eye maple, as shown in the photo at left. The leg-and-apron base is joined with mortises and protruding through tenons. Brass stays hold the lid open to display the inside mirror that can be used when applying makeup. The frame-and-panel case bottom is maple and the compartments contain velvet-lined jewelry trays that are joined with hand-cut dovetails. Quality pervades every aspect of construction and joinery, which can all be done with simple machine setups and enjoyable handwork.

Cutting mortises – Following the dimensions in figure 1, joint and plane the leg stock. Cut the blanks to length, but leave them square until after you've cut their through mortises. Do the same for the aprons, but don't chamfer the bottom edges until you've cut their tenons. I prepared an extra leg and an extra front apron and adjacent side apron to lay out the joints, set up my machines and practice making the tricky mortises and tenons. To resist twisting, the front and back aprons have two through tenons on each end, and each side apron has a ¼-in.-long haunch on either side of its single through tenon. To join the aprons to the top of the leg, the side-apron tenon passes between the front-apron tenons; the short haunches on each side apron don't penetrate the leg deeply enough to touch the cheeks of the front-apron tenons.

Lay out the through mortises for the ⅜-in.-thick by 1-in.-wide tenons from the dimensions in figure 1. The mortise for the single-tenon side apron is on the centerline of the wide face of the legs. And the centerline of each double-tenon front and back apron mortise should be ⁹⁄₁₆ in. from the inside and ¹¹⁄₁₆ in. from the outside of the still-square leg pieces. Each double mortise ends up in the center of the narrower side of each leg after you plane the decorative 3-in. radius shown in figure 1.

Using a horizontal borer, I cut the deep through mortises for the double tenons and the single tenons. (If you don't have a horizontal borer, you can substitute a drill press with a hollow-chisel mortiser or a plunge router.) Then I reset the borer depth and cut the ¼-in.-deep mortise for the side-apron haunch, as shown in the top left photo on p. 109. I used a special rotary miller bit, made by

Drawings: Bob La Pointe

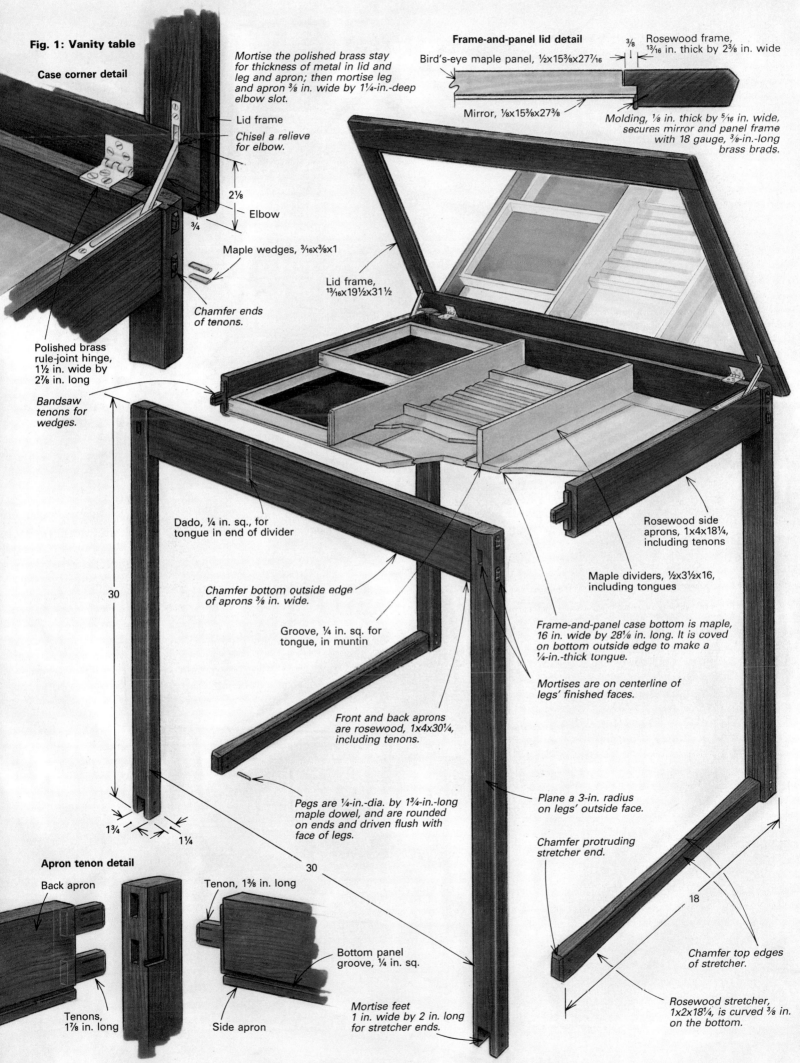

Fig. 1: Vanity table

Case corner detail

Mortise the polished brass stay for thickness of metal in lid and leg and apron; then mortise leg and apron ⅜ in. wide by 1¼-in.-deep elbow slot.

Lid frame

Chisel a relieve for elbow.

2⅛

¾ Elbow

Maple wedges, ³⁄₁₆x⅜x1

Chamfer ends of tenons.

Polished brass rule-joint hinge, 1½ in. wide by 2⅞ in. long

Bandsaw tenons for wedges.

Frame-and-panel lid detail

Bird's-eye maple panel, ½x15⅜x27⁷⁄₁₆

⅜ Rosewood frame, ¹³⁄₁₆ in. thick by 2⅜ in. wide

Mirror, ⅛x15⅜x27⅜

Molding, ⅛ in. thick by ⁵⁄₁₆ in. wide, secures mirror and panel frame with 18 gauge, ⅜-in.-long brass brads.

Lid frame, ¹³⁄₁₆x19½x31½

Dado, ¼ in. sq., for tongue in end of divider

Chamfer bottom outside edge of aprons ⅜ in. wide.

Groove, ¼ in. sq. for tongue, in muntin

Rosewood side aprons, 1x4x18¼, including tenons

Maple dividers, ½x3½x16, including tongues

Frame-and-panel case bottom is maple, 16 in. wide by 28⅛ in. long. It is coved on bottom outside edge to make a ¼-in.-thick tongue.

Mortises are on centerline of legs' finished faces.

Front and back aprons are rosewood, 1x4x30¼, including tenons.

30

30

18

Plane a 3-in. radius on legs' outside face.

Chamfer protruding stretcher end.

Chamfer top edges of stretcher.

Pegs are ¼-in.-dia. by 1¾-in.-long maple dowel, and are rounded on ends and driven flush with face of legs.

1¾   1   1¼

Apron tenon detail

Back apron

Tenon, 1⅜ in. long

Tenons, 1⅞ in. long

Side apron

Bottom panel groove, ¼ in. sq.

Mortise feet 1 in. wide by 2 in. long for stretcher ends.

Rosewood stretcher, 1x2x18¼, is curved ⅜ in. on the bottom.

Inca and available from Garrett Wade Co. Inc., 161 Ave. of the Americas, New York, N.Y. 10013; (212) 807-1155. If you use a borer or router to cut the mortises, square their corners by hand with a chisel. This isn't tedious, since there are only four legs, and I think the experience is therapeutic. Just make sure the chisel is the same size as the mortise and very sharp. Chisel halfway through from the outside of the leg, turn it over and complete the job from the inside of the leg. Finally, to accommodate the dovetail effect of the double-wedged tenons, taper both ends of the mortises. (I'll tell you more about the wedged tenons later.) I tapered the mortises with the same chisel I used for squaring their corners by enlarging the outside openings a little more than 1/16 in. on each end and tapering the walls to the halfway point of each mortise (see the top, center photo on the facing page).

After cutting the mortises in the top of each leg, I handplaned the radius on the outside surface. You need five lines to mark out the radius: a 3-in. arc on each end of the leg, a line running down each side about 1/8 in. below the leg's outside surface to intersect with the arcs and one along the centerline of the face to be radiused. Then handplane the radius to the lines on each side without planing the centerline off, as shown in the top, right photo on the facing page. The irregularities left by the plane can be removed with a scraper and fine-grit sandpaper held on a felt block. There may be faster ways to shape a radius, but since this vanity table isn't a production piece, the intimacy of handwork is a pleasant respite from the incessant roar of machinery. So take the phone off the hook and enjoy your hand tools.

Open mortises in the bottom of the legs accept the stretchers, as shown in figure 1, and are cut with a dado blade on the tablesaw. For safety's sake, I clamped the leg in a tenoning jig, so the radiused surface faces the blade. The mortise dimensions are 1 in. wide and 2 in. long, and the stretchers' chamfered ends protrude through the legs. I finished the stretchers by bandsawing a curve on the bottom edge so that only the ends touch the floor. Then I smoothed the bottom edge and chamfered the top edges with a compass plane.

Cutting the apron tenons—Mark out the 3/8-in.-thick by 1-in.-wide tenons on the extra apron pieces, using the dimensions in figure 1, and use the pieces to set up the tenoning jig and dado blade on the tablesaw. Note that the side-apron tenons are shorter than the front- and back-apron tenons and are offset differently. When the setup is correct, cut the front- and back-apron tenons' outside cheeks 1/4 in. from each apron's outer surface. Then reset the jig and cut the inside cheek 3/8 in. from the inner surface of a test piece. A corner of the resultant test tenon should fit its mortise tightly, and when you're satisfied that it does, cut the cheeks on all the front- and back-apron tenons. Repeat this process for the side aprons (using the extra apron to practice), only this time cut their tenons' outside cheeks 1/8 in. from the outer surface. Then reset the jig and cut the inside cheek 1/2 in. from the inner surface. Again, check that the resultant tenon fits the mortise, and when it does, cut the inside cheeks on all the side-apron tenons.

To cut the tenons to width on the tablesaw, I positioned the pieces against stops on a sliding table and set the dado blade to cut just short of the shoulder, as shown in the bottom, left photo on the facing page. First I cut the 3/8-in.-wide shoulders on both edges of the front and back aprons, and then formed their double tenons by wasting the 1 1/4-in.-wide section between them. You should do this on the extra apron first and check that its tenons fit the mortises before cutting the real aprons. Mark the side aprons' single tenons right on the workpieces (including the extra side apron) and then bandsaw them to width and crosscut their 1/4-in.-long haunches.

Next, I dry-assembled the legs and aprons and scribed a line

around the end of the tenons where they protrude from the mortises, as shown in the center, right photo on the facing page. A block plane works well to chamfer the end of the tenon to this mark. Finally, I bandsawed two kerfs for wedges in each tenon. It isn't essential to wedge the through tenons at the leg-and-apron joints, but the wedges are textural, decorative elements that strengthen the joints and hold them together during glue-up. Start the cuts for the wedges a little more than 1/16 in. from the chamfer in the end of the tenon and stop them at half the tenon length.

To complete the leg-and-apron joinery, I cut a 1/4-in.-sq. groove for the bottom panel 3/8 in. from each apron's lower edge. Then I reassembled the legs and aprons, marked the groove across the legs and chiseled it out so it was continuous from the front and back aprons to the side aprons. Finally, before setting the aprons aside and working on the frame-and-panel case bottom, I planed a 3/8-in.-wide, 45° chamfer on the bottom outside edge of each apron.

Making the frame-and-panel bottom—The vanity's case is portioned into three interior compartments with dividers in the center of the muntins that separate the panels in the case bottom. Each bottom panel is narrow enough to be a single piece of wood. The corners of the bottom frame are slip-jointed and the frame has a 1/4-in.-sq. panel groove in its inside edge. The two muntins have a panel groove on both sides and 1/4x1/4x2 1/2 stub tenons on their ends that fit the groove in the front and back frames. Raise the panels by routing a 1/2-in.-wide cove in their top and bottom edges to leave a 1/4-in.-thick tongue. Now, dry-assemble the frame and panels. When you're satisfied that everything fits, glue and clamp the frame, being careful not to glue the edges of the panels, thereby restricting wood movement.

The top edges of the 3 1/2-in.-wide compartment dividers are 1/8 in. below the upper edges of the aprons. The dividers have a continuous tongue on each end and the bottom edge, which I cut on a shaper using two 1/2-in.-wide cutters with a 1/4-in.-wide collar between them, as shown in the bottom, right photo on the facing page. Then I bandsawed and chiseled a 1/4-in.-wide shoulder on top of the dividers.

When the glue on the frame-and-panel assembly is dry, cove the bottom, outside edge of the frame to leave a 1/4-in.-thick tongue that fits the groove in the aprons. Then rout a 1/4-in.-sq. groove down the center of each muntin for the two compartment dividers. You can do this by guiding a router against a straightedge. To mark out the dado in the aprons for the tongue on the ends of the compartment dividers, assemble the legs and aprons with the bottom and mark where the divider grooves intersect the aprons. Extend these marks up the aprons to 3 in. above the case bottom. After disassembling everything, I cut these dadoes with a plunge router.

Assembling the legs, aprons and bottom—Before assembly, sand everything with fine-grit paper. I'm especially careful to sand areas that would be hard to get at when the vanity is assembled. Then get everything ready for glue-up: the glue, a brush, a damp rag, tenon wedges, and a small hammer to drive them in. It's important to assemble parts systematically and you must work quickly to clamp everything together before the glue dries. You may want to practice with a dry run of each assembly step. I glued up the subassemblies first: the front legs and apron, the back legs and apron, and the case bottom and dividers. Brush a thin coat of glue on the tenons and on the sides of the mortises, but don't apply too much or you'll have an oozy mess. Clamp the joints, brush a light coat of glue on the wedges, and alternately tap each pair home until equal amounts of the wedges are exposed. Since the wedges secure the tenon in the mortise, you can remove the clamps and

Left: The author uses a horizontal borer with a rotary miller bit to cut the through and haunched tenons on the top of a leg.

Center: Moore squares the round mortise left by the horizontal borer and then enlarges the ends and chisels a taper halfway through the mortise to accommodate the "dovetailing" effect of the wedges.

Right: After marking five lines for the radius on the still square leg, the author planes the outside faces.

Left: After cutting the front-apron cheeks with a tenoning jig and dado blade on the tablesaw, Moore wastes the wood between the tenons. He uses a dado blade and a sliding table with stops to limit the space between tenons.

Right: Scribe around each tenon on its still-square ends with a marking knife, holding the knife's flat side against the leg. Chamfer the ends of the tenon to the mark.

Below: Moore cuts the tongue on three sides of a divider on a shaper. He clamps the workpiece on a sliding table and uses two $1/2$-in.-wide cutters with a $1/4$-in.-thick spacer in between.

clean up the squeeze-out. Then glue the dividers to the bottom panel. To ensure even clamping pressure along the length of the divider, clamp with a radiused caul under the bottom panel and keep the divider centered on and square to the panel.

When these subassemblies are dry, assemble the bottom panel to the front legs and aprons. To do this, first glue the divider tongues in the grooves in the apron. I didn't glue the bottom-panel frame to the aprons, but you could, since the grain and wood movement of the frame and aprons run in the same direction. Next, glue the side-apron tenons to the mortises in the front legs, and glue the back subassembly to the side aprons and dividers. Clamp the case from front to back, wedge the tenons, and then clean up the squeeze-out. Finally, handsaw the wedges flush with the protruding ends of the tenons.

When the leg-and-apron assembly is dry, turn the table upside down and glue the stretchers to the bottom of the legs. The stretcher ends should protrude evenly in front and back. Clamp across each joint and let the glue dry before you peg the joints. For pegs, I used two ¼-in.-dia. by 1¾-in.-long maple dowels with radiused ends that are flush with the leg's surface when driven in.

Building and hanging the lid—The lid's East Indian rosewood frame is secured with a slip joint, which I cut on the tablesaw with a tenoning jig and dado blade. After assembling the frame, chamfer its top and bottom outside edges and then rout a ⅜-in.-wide by ⁹⁄₁₆-in.-deep rabbet in its inside edges for the panel and mirror. Since the mirror may have to be replaced, I secured it and the panel to the frame with a nailed in, removable molding. I resawed and book-matched two pieces of bird's-eye maple for the ½-in.-thick panel, and after gluing it up and cutting it to size, I routed a ¼-in.-sq. rabbet in its top edge. The resultant tongue should lap the tongue in the frame's rabbet and leave the panel's top surface flush with the face of the frame.

Before installing the mirror and top panel, hang the lid on the base with hinges and install the stays. The pivot point of the hinge must be beyond the leg to prevent the lid's ¾-in. overhang from binding when the lid is opened. You could use wide butt hinges for this, but instead I hung the lid on 1½-in.-wide by 2⅞-in.-long rule-joint hinges (available from most woodworking-supply catalogs). On these hinges, one leaf is longer than the other and this extends the pivot point beyond the legs. However, I used the hinges upside down so the knuckle would be up, making it unnecessary to mortise the knuckle into the bottom of the lid. To reverse the hinge, I countersunk the screw holes in its back and polished those new visible faces. Then, with the hinge edges flush on the inside edge of the back apron, I scribed the placement of the long leaves with a marking knife and cut the mortise with a sharp chisel. To mark the hinge placement in the lid frame, temporarily fasten both hinges in the apron and set the lid in place. Ensure that its overhang is uniform all around, and then scribe the location of the hinges in the lid frame. Remove the hinges, hold them against the scribe marks and extend the marks around the hinge. Finally, mortise the hinges into the lid frame.

I used lid stays that are milled from solid brass. (I bought mine from Jack Dale, 18299 Mariposa Creek Road, Willits, Cal. 95490; 707-485-8251.) These stays are strong, and since they are mortised into the side aprons and lid frame, no part of them is on the inside of the aprons, which could interfere with the jewelry trays. The instructions that come with each set of stays assumes that the back of the lid is flush with the back legs. Since there's a ¾-in. overhang, you must install them according to the dimensions in figure 1 to ensure they will be flush with the leg. I recommend that you practice on a mock-up lid and apron. I plunge-routed the mortises for the stay into the lid and apron by guiding the router's fence against a strip of wood taped onto the apron.

Before permanently screwing the hardware in place, I polished it (including the screw heads) on a buffing wheel and applied four coats of lacquer to the wood and rubbed it out to a high sheen. Since the panel is removable, you can lacquer it before assembly and then secure it and the mirror in the lid frame. Drill holes for small brass brads and gently nail the molding in place.

Making the jewelry and cosmetic trays—The case's middle compartment is for cosmetics and tissues. I attached a grooved board to a piece of maple, which fits loosely in the compartment. The grooves, which are routed across the width of the board, hold eyeliner pencils, lipsticks and other makeup items. The best way to customize the storage compartments is to check with the client before making them. Each side compartment has two removable jewelry trays: both are half the depth of the compartment, but one is the same size as the compartment and one is half its length. The smaller tray slides from front to back on top of the lower box so you can access the jewelry in the bottom tray. I dovetailed the ⁵⁄₁₆-in.-thick by 1½-in.-high tray sides and grooved them for a ¼-in.-thick maple plywood bottom, which I covered with black velvet.

Making the stool—The stool (shown in figure 2 at left) is simply a miniature of the vanity table. All the details are the same, except that I used blind tenons, instead of wedged through tenons, for the leg-and-apron joints. The seat of the stool is similar to the lid of the table, except that it doesn't open. It's fastened to the grooves in the aprons with wooden cabinetmaker's buttons. □

Terry Moore has been a professional furnituremaker in Newport, N.H., for 15 years. In 1986, The League of New Hampshire Craftsmen awarded this vanity Best in Show during its annual juried exhibit.

Fig. 2: Stool
All stool parts are rosewood except where noted.

Detail: Section view of frame and panel

Panel

Tongue, ¼ in. wide by ⅜ in. deep

Frame

Seat frame, ¹³⁄₁₆ in. thick by 2 in. wide

Bird's-eye maple seat panel, ½x10¼x16¼

Seat measures 13½ in. wide by 19½ in. long.

17

Side aprons, ⅞x3x11, including tenons

Front and back aprons, ⅞x3x16, including tenons

Pegs

18

12

Legs, 1x1½x16³⁄₁₆

Stretchers, ⅞x1½x12¼

Index